"I love this book! It is nearly i

practical, pastoral wisdom that

be a pastor is a high honor, and being commissioned to preach the gospel is a beautiful thing, but the life of a pastor always includes seasons of hardship. Each chapter of this book speaks into those seasons with the tenderness of compassion, the grace of understanding, and the helpfulness of truth spoken in love. If you are a pastor, get this book, read it with an open heart, and then keep it near, because there will be seasons when you will reach for it again and find it to be your friend."

Paul David Tripp, President, Paul Tripp Ministries; author, *New Morning Mercies* and *Suffering*

"In ministry, you need company—and the wiser the company, the better. Not all of us enjoy mutually encouraging pastoral friendships with the likes of the contributors to this volume, but here they welcome you into their own lives and experiences and doubts and heartbreaks and trials. In so doing, they offer counsel and hope for those in ministry. And we all need that."

J. Ligon Duncan III, Chancellor, CEO, and John E. Richards Professor of Systematic and Historical Theology, Reformed Theological Seminary

"Pastors get worn down, discouraged, depleted, and depressed. This short but pastorally rich book will prove to be a spiritual tonic for pastors. I recommend reading and meditating on the essays in this book, which will provide strength and solace for the journey."

Thomas R. Schreiner, James Buchanan Harrison Professor of New Testament Interpretation, The Southern Baptist Theological Seminary

"The apostle Paul wrote, 'Follow me, as I follow Christ.' We grow not only by learning true concepts but also by following faithful people. In *Faithful Endurance*, a team of veteran pastors invites younger pastors to follow them into the buffetings and temptations of ministry, offering the path of wisdom that the Lord faithfully provides for every new generation. I wish this fine book had been available to me when I was a young pastor."

Ray Ortlund, Senior Pastor, Immanuel Church, Nashville, Tennessee

"Pastoral ministry often feels like a labyrinth filled with uncertain turns and innumerable blind spots. If ventured on alone, the journey is marked by constant frustration and despair. But if you are joined by a friend, especially a wise one, the journey is not only more enjoyable but also more likely to result in safe passage. While reading *Faithful Endurance,* I felt accompanied by wise friends who imparted insightful wisdom that I trust will help me and any other pastor to remain faithful until the end."

Garrett Kell, Lead Pastor, Del Ray Baptist Church, Alexandria, Virginia

"Many pastors face unanticipated troubles—ministry discouragement, constant criticism, devotional dryness, or feelings of inadequacy and failure. They need seasoned leaders to speak directly to them in the midst of these challenging situations. And they need these leaders to share the wisdom they've learned from God's Word and their own similar experiences. In other words, they need the stabilizing encouragement of this book. I wish I had had it years ago, and I gladly commend it to fellow pastors."

Drew Hunter, Teaching Pastor, Zionsville Fellowship, Zionsville, Indiana; author, *Made for Friendship*

Faithful Endurance

Other Gospel Coalition Books

Coming Home: Essays on the New Heaven and New Earth, edited by D. A. Carson and Jeff Robinson Sr.

Don't Call It a Comeback: The Old Faith for a New Day, edited by Kevin DeYoung

15 Things Seminary Couldn't Teach Me, edited by Collin Hansen and Jeff Robinson

Glory in the Ordinary: Why Your Work in the Home Matters to God, by Courtney Reissig

God's Love Compels Us: Taking the Gospel to the World, edited by D. A. Carson and Kathleen B. Nielson

God's Word, Our Story: Learning from the Book of Nehemiah, edited by D. A. Carson and Kathleen B. Nielson

The Gospel as Center: Renewing Our Faith and Reforming Our Ministry Practices, edited by D. A. Carson and Timothy Keller

Gospel-Centered Youth Ministry: A Practical Guide, edited by Cameron Cole and Jon Nielson

Here Is Our God: God's Revelation of Himself in Scripture, edited by Kathleen B. Nielson and D. A. Carson

His Mission: Jesus in the Gospel of Luke, edited by D. A. Carson and Kathleen B. Nielson

Joyfully Spreading the Word, edited by Kathleen Nielson and Gloria Furman

Missional Motherhood, by Gloria Furman

The New City Catechism: 52 Questions and Answers for Our Hearts and Minds

The New City Catechism Curriculum

The New City Catechism Devotional: God's Truth for Our Hearts and Minds

The New City Catechism for Kids

The Pastor as Scholar and the Scholar as Pastor: Reflections on Life and Ministry, by John Piper and D. A. Carson, edited by David Mathis and Owen Strachan

Praying Together: The Priority and Privilege of Prayer; In Our Homes, Communities, and Churches, by Megan Hill

Pursuing Health in an Anxious Age, by Bob Cutillo

Remember Death, by Matthew McCullough

Resurrection Life in a World of Suffering, edited by D. A. Carson and Kathleen Nielson

The Scriptures Testify about Me: Jesus and the Gospel in the Old Testament, edited by D. A. Carson

Seasons of Waiting: Walking by Faith When Dreams Are Delayed, by Betsy Childs Howard

Word-Filled Women's Ministry: Loving and Serving the Church, edited by Gloria Furman and Kathleen B. Nielson

Faithful Endurance

The Joy of Shepherding People for a Lifetime

Edited by Collin Hansen
and Jeff Robinson Sr.

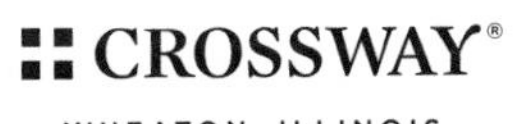

WHEATON, ILLINOIS

Faithful Endurance: The Joy of Shepherding People for a Lifetime

Published by Crossway
1300 Crescent Street
Wheaton, Illinois 60187

Cover design: Peter Voth, @petervoth

First printing 2019

Printed in the United States of America

All emphases in Scripture quotations have been added by the author.

Trade paperback ISBN: 978-1-4335-6265-5
ePub ISBN: 978-1-4335-6268-6
PDF ISBN: 978-1-4335-6266-2
Mobipocket ISBN: 978-1-4335-6267-9

Library of Congress Cataloging-in-Publication Data

Names: Hansen, Collin, 1981–editor.
Title: Faithful endurance : the joy of shepherding people for a lifetime / edited by Collin Hansen and Jeff Robinson Sr.
Description: Wheaton : Crossway, 2019. | Series: The gospel coalition | Includes bibliographical references and index.
Identifiers: LCCN 2018038860 (print) | LCCN 2018053993 (ebook) | ISBN 9781433562662 (pdf) | ISBN 9781433562679 (mobi) | ISBN 9781433562686 (epub) | ISBN 9781433562655 (tp)
Subjects: LCSH: Pastoral theology.
Classification: LCC BV4011.3 (ebook) | LCC BV4011.3 .F35 2019 (print) | DDC 253/.2—dc23
LC record available at https://lccn.loc.gov/2018038860

Crossway is a publishing ministry of Good News Publishers.

VP 28 27 26 25 24 23 22 21 20 19
15 14 13 12 11 10 9 8 7 6 5 4 3 2 1

For my pastors—
may God grant us strength and faith
to finish the race together.

Collin Hansen

For Harry Reeder and Tony Rose,
two ministry heroes who have shown me what it means
to endure in faithfulness over the long haul
through many dangers, toils, and snares.

Jeff Robinson Sr.

Contents

Introduction

Collin Hansen

Pastors and other elders have been called to one task not entrusted to every Christian—teaching. But in other ways the path of faithful endurance in following Christ looks the same for the shepherds as for the sheep. And that means that Jesus calls them to do what he did for them. The Good Shepherd lays down his life for the sheep (John 10:11, 15) so that he may take it up again (10:17). Indeed, "greater love has no one than this, that someone lay down his life for his friends" (15:13).

Peter, that rock upon which Christ promised to build his church (Matt. 16:18), neither understood nor initially agreed with Jesus on this point. When Jesus told him that the Christ must suffer many things, including death, Peter rebuked him. But Jesus rebuked him in return, going so far as to call him Satan, the accuser or adversary (16:21–23). Jesus explained to a crowd, to Peter, and to his other disciples what enduring faithfulness looks like: "If anyone would come after me, let him deny himself and take up his cross and follow me. For whoever would save his life will lose it, but whoever loses his life for my sake and the gospel's will save it" (Mark 8:34–35). Even then, when Peter promised Jesus that he would lay down his life for his friend, Jesus knew better: "Truly, truly, I say to you, the rooster will not crow till you have denied me three times" (John 13:37–38).

But Jesus restored his friend Peter. And by his death and resurrection he restores us also, to fellowship with God and to service in his church. Apart from Jesus we can do nothing (John 15:5). In him, though, we are more than conquerors (Rom. 8:37) on the march to heaven. One day we will see the Shepherd of our souls face to face (1 Cor. 13:12).

Until then, Jesus tells us what direction the road of faithful endurance will take us—for all of us as Christians, not least those of us who lead the church. We give our soul, our life, our all. This sacrifice is the essence of love, as the apostle John taught us: "By this we know love, that he laid down his life for us, and we ought to lay down our lives for the brothers" (1 John 3:16).

The essays in this book will help you walk that road of sacrificial love with confidence and joy. It is a profound responsibility to shepherd people for a lifetime. Each chapter begins with a question that reflects a scenario commonly faced by pastors. And the answer, from a veteran pastor, seeks to apply godly wisdom in response. We hope that this dialogue will help you "run with endurance the race that is set before us" by "looking to Jesus, the founder and perfecter of our faith, who for the joy that was set before him endured the cross, despising the shame, and is seated at the right hand of the throne of God" (Heb. 12:1–2).

1

Ministry Has Left Me Spiritually Listless

Tim Keller

Dear Pastor Tim,

Last Sunday I was struck by Paul's words in Philippians 4 that he had learned the secret to contentment. The Lord has given me a great place to serve, and I think it's going reasonably well. I enjoy the deep study of Scripture that comes with preaching every week, and I probably spend at least fifty hours per week on church work.

I continue to grow in my knowledge of the things of God, but my devotional life is lifeless. I'm just not content. I fret a lot over things, especially whether the church is flourishing under my leadership, whether I'm working hard enough, and whether I know enough. I'll admit that though things are going well at the church, I'm not thrilled that other churches around us are growing while we seem to have plateaued. The church has done fairly well under my leadership, but to be frank, I expected more.

Yes, I realize I have much to be content over, but no amount of "success" ever seems to do it for me. Why am I feeling this way? What has left me feeling so listless, even subtly bitter?

Faithfully your friend,

Discontented Shepherd

Dear Discontented Shepherd,[1]

I spent forty-two years in ordained vocational ministry. Many who started with me didn't get to the finish line. It's a grievous percentage. One of the main reasons so many didn't last, I think, is because no one warned them about the ways ministry can tempt one with pride.

This is where Paul's words in 2 Corinthians 12:7–10 have been so helpful to me as a pastor. Paul—the very apostle trained in theology and for ministry by the actual risen Christ—warns us that theological training and life in ministry can lead to conceit if you fail to cooperate with Christ's gracious intervention:

> So to keep me from becoming conceited because of the surpassing greatness of the revelations, a thorn was given me in the flesh, a messenger of Satan to harass me, to keep me from becoming conceited. Three times I pleaded with the Lord about this, that it should leave me. But he said to me, "My grace is sufficient for you, for my power is made perfect in weakness." Therefore I will boast all the more gladly of my weaknesses, so that the power of Christ may rest upon me. For the sake of Christ, then, I am content with weaknesses,

1. This chapter is adapted from Tim Keller, "3 Ways Ministry Can Make You Conceited," The Gospel Coalition, July 5, 2017, https://www.thegospelcoalition.org/article/3-ways-ministry-can-make-you-conceited/. Used by permission of the author.

> insults, hardships, persecutions, and calamities. For when I am weak, then I am strong.

Here are three ways ministry can make you conceited unless God intervenes. Be warned.

Theological Knowledge Can Puff You Up

First, there's the conceit of theological knowledge. Now you might think, *It's a stretch to say Paul is arguing that theological knowledge leads to conceit.* But elsewhere he says, "We know that 'We all possess knowledge.' But knowledge puffs up while love builds up. Those who think they know something do not yet know as they ought to know" (1 Cor. 8:1–2 NIV).

Here he's explicitly talking about theological knowledge. Some in Corinth had the right theological knowledge about meat offered to idols, but what did it lead to? Being puffed up. He's saying something simple. Knowing the truth has a tendency to inflate you. You become self-involved, proud of your knowledge and insight. Love, on the other hand, is self-emptying. Love is saying, "Your needs are more important than mine." But being puffed up means that you become more self-involved, you become proud, you become proud of your knowledge, you become proud of your insight. And Paul says that it doesn't have to be that way, but the fact is that it very often is.

In his exposition of Ephesians 6, I think the words of D. Martyn Lloyd-Jones are helpful:

> Whenever you allow your relationship to the truth to become purely theoretical and academic, you're falling into the grip of Satan. . . .
>
> The moment in your study you cease to come under the power of the truth, you have become a victim of the Devil. If you can study the Bible without being searched and examined and humbled, without being lifted up and made to praise God, or moved with sorrow over what God has endured in you, or amazed at the beauty and wisdom of what Christ has done for

> you, if you do not feel as much of a desire to sing when you're alone in your study as when you're standing in the pulpit, you are in bad shape. And you should always feel something in this power.[2]

Lloyd-Jones proceeds to identify the marks of someone who has learned to master the Bible as a set of mere information, not extraordinary power. One mark is that you become a spiritual crank. A spiritual crank is someone always complaining about relatively fine shades of doctrinal distinctions, always denouncing others in arguments over Bible translations or denouncing people on the wrong side of the latest theological controversy. A spiritual crank treats the Word of God as something you use, not something that uses you. He's puffed up on intellectual pride and his theological tribe.

Ministry Can Become a False Identity

The second conceit comes from a false identity created by ministry. You will tend to identify personally with your ministry so much so that its success (or lack thereof) becomes your success (or lack thereof). Once you begin to identify in this way, you'll create a false identity based on your performance as a minister. If you don't understand this point, it will be one of your main battlegrounds in the years ahead. What do I mean by false identity?

It can manifest itself in at least four ways:

1. *Success*: Any of us can build a false identity based on circumstances and performance. Every single Christian struggles with a false identity. Every non-Christian has a false identity. Those of us in full-time ministry will face the sting of success one way or another. When people come to your church, you're going to feel like they are affirming you, and when people leave your church, you're going to feel like it's a personal attack.

2. D. Martyn Lloyd-Jones, "'Knowledge Puffeth Up,'" in *The Christian Warfare: An Exposition of Ephesians 6:10–13* (Grand Rapids, MI: Baker, 1976), 180.

2. *Criticism*: If your ministry becomes your false identity, you won't be able to handle criticism. Criticism will come and be so traumatic, because it questions how good a pastor you are. Criticism says, "You know, your preaching really isn't very good. . . . I want my preacher to be better." It feels like a personal attack. The criticism either devastates you, or you dismiss it and don't grow from it.
3. *Cowardice*: If your ministry becomes your false identity, you will succumb to cowardice. There are two kinds of cowardice. There's true cowardice—being afraid to rock the boat or to offend the people who give the most money to the church or to preach a word that turns young people off. That's true cowardice. But there's another kind of cowardice that I call "counterfeit" cowardice. This is the cowardice of being too abrasive, of being too harsh, of running people off and then saying, "See, I'm valiant for truth." This also comes from identifying with your ministry.
4. *Comparisons*: One last sign that you've fallen into a false identity is that you cannot stand comparisons. You get envious when you see others succeeding because you don't think they work as hard as you do or are not as theologically astute as you are. Everything is coming up roses for them in their ministry, and that bothers you.

Pastor, there's nothing worse than identifying with your ministry. And by the way, if you don't think that's going be a lifelong struggle, you don't know your own heart.

Ministry Can Make You Outwardly Focused

When you speak to people about God, you have two options: commune with God, or act like you commune with God. Since the minister's job is to tell people how great God is and how wonderful the Christian life can be, his life needs to reflect it. So you either have to be close to God as you minister, or you have to act close to God. Either you truly learn how to commune with God, or you learn how to fake it: you talk as if you're a lot closer to God than you actually are. And not only do people start to think that, but you start to think it too. This can be devastating for your heart. That's what is so horribly dangerous about ministry.

On Jesus's last night with the disciples, he said one of them would betray him (John 13:21). It's interesting to consider how the disciples responded. They all looked around and asked who this person was. In fact, after Jesus told them that it was the one he would give bread to, they still didn't get it. You know why? Because Judas didn't look any different than they did. Outwardly, he was an effective minister, but inwardly, there was nothing there. He took care of his outward life more than his inward life. Jonathan Edwards, in his great book *Charity and Its Fruits*, talks about the fact that God used Judas even though he wasn't saved. We don't want that to be our legacy in ministry.

But here's where hypocrisy starts. Ministry is either going to make you a far better Christian or a far worse Christian than you would have otherwise been. It's going to make you a hard, pharisaical hypocrite, or it's going to turn you into a softer, more tender person, because it forces you to go to the throne of grace and to beg the Lord for help in your weakness. The ministry will either drive you to him or drive you away from him. Like Judas, you choose what life you care for.

Overcome Your Conceits

So how do we overcome these conceits? Remember Paul's situation in 2 Corinthians. He's facing false apostles and teachers who are saying he doesn't have the credentials to be a true apostle. Paul counters that he does have the credentials—but not the kind we would expect. He inverts all the categories. Instead of boasting about his theological knowledge, great success, or picture-perfect outward life, he boasts in insults, hardships, and being run out of town on a rail.

This is how he contends that God is truly with him. He tells us to look at all the things God has done to bring him to his knees.

Pastor, consider all the things God has done to break your pride. Look at all the ways he has brought you to the end of yourself so that you would cling to him more tightly. Let all your failures and disappointments and weaknesses drive you like a nail into the love of God. Only by embracing them will you ever become a true minister and make it to the finish line.

2

Is It Time for Me to Go?

D. A. Carson

Dear Pastor Don,

I am writing to let you know that I may have reached the end of my rope at this church and stand in desperate need of your advice. I've been pastoring here for the past forty years and am nearly convinced that perhaps this church's future is not my future. I'm wondering if I should leave or retire. I think the evidence is fairly strong. I've been praying for wisdom, but so far, God has provided me with no clear path forward.

I don't have much gas in the tank of energy when it comes to leadership or preaching. I'm tired, frustrated, and discouraged. Please understand, there are no moral problems. My devotional life remains robust, and there is no hidden sin that would disqualify me. I still love to read good works of theology and church history—mixed in, of course, with a little Marilynne Robinson and Wendell Berry now and then. I simply think it may be time for me to move on for my own good and the betterment of the church. Maybe I've done all I can for my flock. Have I already stayed too long? I've seen other pastors do it even though the handwriting was on the wall. I don't want to do that. It weakens the church and dishonors God when we stay simply because we don't know what else to do.

Please advise. Am I out of bounds biblically, theologically, or ethically? When do you think it wise for a man to consider moving on to another theater of gospel service? I eagerly await your counsel.

Faithfully,

Hanging On Too Long

Dear Hanging On Too Long,[1]

Certain kinds of questions come my way by email fairly regularly—every few weeks, every couple of months. This is not an unusual question, and circumstances that make a man ponder leaving his current place of service are not rare, so I'm not at all taken aback by your question.

When a young pastor asks this question, it is usually prompted by a difficult situation he longs to flee. But it's quite different when a man is in his late fifties, sixties, or seventies. I think you would agree that the first question to ask is this: Are there any biblical and theological principles that should shape our reflection on these matters?

Valid Question

In one sense, you have phrased the question in the right way. You have not reached some long-awaited ideal retirement age and are now looking for an excuse to withdraw from ministry in favor of buying an RV to spend the next couple of decades alternating between fishing lakes and visits to grandchildren. After all, there is no well-articulated theology of retirement in Scripture. Rather, this is a serious question from someone who has borne the heat of the day

1. This chapter is adapted from D. A. Carson, "On Knowing When to Resign," *Themelios* 42, no. 2 (2017): 255–58. Used by permission of the author.

and who, for various reasons, wonders if it is not only permitted but right to ask if it is time to move on.

In recent years, I've been passing on what I've picked up from a few senior saints who have thought these things through. The most important lesson is this: provided one does not succumb to cancer, Alzheimer's, or any other seriously debilitating disease, the first thing we have to confront as we get older is declining energy levels.

Moreover, by "declining energy levels," I am referring not only to the kind of declining physical reserves that demand more rest and fewer hours of labor each week but also to declining emotional energy, without which it is difficult to cope with a full panoply of pastoral pressures. When those energy levels begin to fall is hugely variable (at age forty-five? Sixty-five? Seventy-five?), as is also how fast they fall. But fall they will! It follows that if one attempts at age eighty-five to do what one managed to accomplish at age forty-five, a lot of it will be done badly. Frustrations commonly follow: old-man crankiness, rising resentments against the younger generation, a tendency to look backward and become defensive, even an unwitting destruction of what one has spent a lifetime building up.

Major Considerations

I mention three major considerations. I hope these provide some guidance.

First, as long as God provides stable energy levels, one should resist the glitter of common secular assumptions about retirement—for example, that there is (or should be) a universal retirement age, that somehow your work entitles you to a retirement free from all service, that the end of life should be dominated by pleasurable pastimes emptied of self-sacrifice and service. This is not to argue that there is no place for, say, time devoted to creative tasks of one sort or another; it is to argue that it is sub-Christian to imagine that our service across the decades entitles us to a carefree retirement.

Second, once energy levels start to decline (whenever that might be), then, assuming neither senility nor some other chronic disease is taking its toll, the part of wisdom is to stop doing some things so that, with one's limited energy, one can tackle the remaining things with enthusiasm and gusto. I can think of two or three senior saints who have become wholly admirable models in this regard. In their late sixties, they slowly started to put aside one task after another, with the result that, now in their early nineties, they can still do the one or two remaining things exceptionally well. One of them, for instance, will still preach but never more than once a day. And he won't fly anywhere: he travels to the place where he is to preach either by car (with someone driving him) or by train. But when he does preach, you can close your eyes and listen to a man who sounds thirty or forty years younger.

There is a third element in such decisions that is partly subjective, partly temperamental, partly a reflection of one's sense of call—and of the ways these various factors interact with one another. John Calvin died on May 27, 1564, at the age of fifty-four. All his life he held himself to the most rigorous, punishing schedule. On the one hand, that stunning self-discipline, a reflection of his passion for the glory of God and for the promotion of the gospel, was used by God to make the man astonishingly productive. On the other hand, all the biographies I have read of him speculate that if in his latter years he had slowed down a little, he might have lived a good deal longer—and had he lived another decade or two, still with stable health, he may well have produced a great deal more. But who are we to tell John Calvin what he should have done?

Human motives are usually mixed. On the one hand, there is something hauntingly exemplary about a person who wants to burn out for Christ, to waste no time, to serve others, as Rudyard Kipling put it, to "fill the unforgiving minute / With sixty seconds' worth of distance run"; on the other hand, there may be a wee touch of workaholism in such a stance, in which our self-identity is tied to the number of hours we put in or the number of things we produce.

It might be a careful and thoughtful stewarding of our declining energies that makes a wise calculation about dropping certain responsibilities so as to maintain more important priorities, but who is to deny that there may also be a touch of entitlement, or a cooling of youthful ardor, a dangerous love of mere ease? Each of us will have to give an answer to our beloved Master, who knows us better than we do. It is probably not too much to suggest that if we are temperamentally drawn to one or the other of these extremes, we should be especially diligent to explore our motives most carefully.

Seven Important Conditions

Finally, all things being equal (and of course, they never are), one should not leave one's ministry until one or more of the following conditions is met:

1. One has to leave for moral reasons. Sadly, such failures are not restricted to young pastors. The older one gets, the more one should pray for grace to finish well.
2. Serious health issues mean that one can no longer discharge one's pastoral duties fruitfully, leaving no realistic hope of returning to full strength.
3. One is clearly called by God to some other ministry. In this case, all the usual complex factors have to be borne in mind.
4. One judges that it would be a good thing for this ministry if the baton were passed to a younger leader in an orderly way. There is no absolute rule, but the rule of thumb is that the longer a person has stayed in one ministry, and the more fruitful that person has been, the wiser it is for that pastor to help arrange the transition to a successor before bowing out. It is not hard to think of exceptions, of course: for example, an old man merely trying to deploy a bit of nepotism or control the future while neither consulting anyone nor using the transition to train church leaders. Generally, however, the rule of thumb proves valuable.
5. One senses one's energy levels are declining, and it seems wise to let go of some responsibilities so that one can the more faithfully discharge remaining responsibilities. In some cases

that can most easily and fruitfully be worked out by taking on a reduced load in the church, while someone else steps up to the primary leadership; in other cases, the only way to opt for reduced responsibilities is by resigning from that charge and taking on a smaller and different assignment.

6. Sometimes one must relinquish one's position and work because of the declining health of a spouse. I have known several pastors who reduced their work dramatically and finally resigned from the pastorate to look after a spouse suffering from advanced dementia.
7. The final condition that may justify leaving one's ministry is precipitated by a developing crisis. In some instances, pressures build up among the elders that reflect differences in vision and priorities. These disparate visions may harden into deeply opposed camps. One may argue that the situation should not have been allowed to develop so far—but there it is. At their worst, such situations are extraordinarily difficult for outsiders to analyze accurately. Has the problem arisen primarily because one or two elders are power hungry and want to become ecclesiastical bosses—people who, quite frankly, need to face discipline? Or because a senior pastor has become entrenched in the conviction that he is always right and has nothing to learn from anyone? Or is it a case of a Barnabas and a Paul unable to reach an amicable agreement on a pastoral issue, where both sides feel strongly and can marshal compelling arguments? In some instances of this sort, one should not step down but should try and sort it out before walking away and leaving a potential mess to a successor. But in other instances, one should resign, conscious of the fact that the differences of opinion, while deep, are not about orthodoxy or morality and that the strong action that would be necessary to restore unanimity among the elders is likely to split the church for little if any gospel gain. In such cases, it may be best simply to step aside with humility and grace, committing the elders and the church to the grace of God.

No Formulaic Answer

The frequency with which pastors move from local church ministry to itinerant ministry is a topic that deserves more study than it has received. Clearly, this can be a wise move. I know former pastors and professors who "retired" into carefully selected teaching ministry in the Two-Thirds World, where their years of accumulated experience benefit many people who do not otherwise have ready access to excellent teaching. Others fruitfully take on a series of interim ministries, where the fixed end of the interim period greatly reduces the stress but provides an opportunity to offer strategic help. Many others set up independent nonprofit organizations that specialize in niche ministries—on the family, for instance, or on repentance and holiness. Many of these nonprofits solicit funds to support the ministry. The former pastor becomes a niche guru on the selected topic.

It would be both uncharitable and mischievous to suggest that all this is intrinsically bad. But it would be naïve not to perceive that there are some dangers to these developments. Some forms of itinerant ministry generate indolence: you preach the same "package" wherever you go, with the result that you quit studying and growing in your knowledge of Holy Scripture and in your ability to teach parts of it you've never taught before. Being a guest preacher tends to garner thanks and commendations without the criticism and rebukes that regular ministry in a local church or seminary tend to provide as a counterbalance—and an exclusive diet of praise is not good for anyone. In short, sometimes itinerant ministry appears to be green grass on the other side of the fence, with too little awareness of the rattlers lurking in the undergrowth. As always, there is great value in testing our motives.

What all this boils down to is that there is no formulaic answer for you to the question, How do I know when it is time to resign? Nevertheless, there are some guidelines that many find helpful, guidelines bound up with the glory of the gospel, the primacy of the local church, the honesty to admit when we are aging, the urgency of training up the next generation, the passion to glorify Christ in our senior years, and the hunger to teach the whole counsel of God.

3

My Preaching Always Sounds the Same

Bryan Chapell

Dear Pastor Bryan,

I'm in a preaching slump. It seems that every week, no matter what passage of Scripture I'm working from, the sermon always sounds the same—three points and a poem. I don't know if my congregation has grown tired of my preaching, but I'm wearied by it. It seems like every book I preach, whether it's 2 Corinthians or 2 Chronicles, my sermons give the people a few major points and some tired, general application. What should I do? How do you preach expository sermons from, say, Daniel or Ruth without sounding moralistic or preaching it as if it were Colossians or Romans?

Thus far, my congregation has been long-suffering, but I know it must sound like "the same old, same old" every Lord's Day. Any advice on how to keep it fresh? How to preach historical narrative differently than I do the Pastoral Epistles? I would appreciate your sage wisdom, and I know my congregation would as well.

Blessings in Christ,

Bored with Myself

Dear Bored with Myself,

I can certainly relate to your concern. An old anecdote tells of a preacher who repeated the same sermon for three Sundays in a row. Fearing a fourth iteration, church elders asked for an explanation. Said the preacher, "When you finish doing what this text requires, I'll move on to the next." The laugh may cut a bit too close to the bone for listeners who sense that our sermons "all sound the same."

Those who study denominations such as the one I serve (evangelical, largely Anglo, suburban, and middle class) say that the sermons of our preachers most commonly address the "3M" concerns of church culture: morals, marriage, and money. When we break from those themes, the most common subjects (often related to the 3Ms) are the 3Ps: politics, pro-life, and propagation (the last often addressed under the headings of mission, discipleship, and evangelism). These subjects are certainly worthy of scriptural address, but they obviously don't cover the scope of Scripture's subjects or the concerns of Christian brothers and sisters across our nation and world with different demographics, circumstances, and priorities.

If familiar themes are constantly preached—and they will vary from church to church—the pastor may be addressing issues most relevant to his people. But he also might be unwittingly serving the perceived priorities of his people rather than the priorities of Scripture. Long ago, thoughtful reformers taught that the preacher's goal is to address "the necessities and capacities" of hearers.[1] We must not settle for addressing only subjects that our people have a ready capacity to hear (or that we find easy to address); biblical preachers are also obligated to preach what God's people need to hear to be conformed to Christ in all of life.

How do we break the preoccupations of our preaching that not only dull hearers to our messages but also blind them to the implications of the lordship of Christ over the whole of life? Here we expand our subject zones when we understand that variety in preaching is more than a marketing gimmick; it's a pastoral and biblical necessity for those who won't hesitate to preach the whole counsel of God.

Expand Your Subject Variety

You must exegete both your texts and your listeners.

The expositor's ethic to "say what the text says" automatically expands our subject categories if we preach consecutively (i.e., covering texts and subjects as they arise in the course of preaching through books of the Bible). John A. Broadus, the father of modern expository preaching, wisely noted that preaching through books of the Bible (even if we do not advance verse by verse) necessarily leads to preaching subjects not otherwise considered by the pastor.[2] Consecutive preaching also naturally brings subjects before the congregation that might not otherwise be tolerated by listeners if the subjects seem to be chosen topically by the pastor to "pick on" someone or some community practice.

Expository preaching doesn't rule out the wisdom of topical sermons or a series that addresses a particular need of a congregation or community. The expositor who insists on plowing through all sixty-six chapters of Isaiah—despite a community crisis, family needs, or a congregation worn out on the themes addressed by the prophet—isn't expounding the congregation as well as the text. All

1. Westminster Larger Catechism, q. 159.
2. John A. Broadus, *On the Preparation and Delivery of Sermons*, ed. Jesse B. Weatherspoon, rev. ed. (1870; repr., New York: Harper & Row, 1944), 142.

preachers are obligated to exegete listeners as well as texts: (1) What do they need to hear? (2) What are they capable of hearing? (3) How long will they be here? Failure to do this "listener exegesis" under the maxim "I prioritize the text" discloses a misunderstanding of pastoral responsibilities. We don't serve the principles of our text by speaking in ways that the text cannot reasonably be heard or that do not allow an appropriate variety of texts to be heard.

Look Forward and Backward

If a pastor is in a mobile community (e.g., in churches dominated by college students, military personnel, or adults early in their career) or one in which youth or families are quickly maturing, then determining a curriculum of subjects needed to equip congregants for the scope of life issues is vital.[3] Sticking to long expository series from books that are not expansive in their subject coverage hinders the necessary life preparation. It's possible to be a sound expositor by dealing with particular topics (e.g., marriage, racism, civility, career choice, stewardship) in an expository way (i.e., going verse by verse through texts where those subjects are addressed), rather than automatically making every sermon series cover an entire book.

Whether we're considering what subjects a sermon series should cover or what book to expound, wise preachers look backward and forward—considering subjects they've covered in recent months or years and also subjects that should be covered to equip listeners for the complexities and challenges of future godly living.

Many preachers find it helpful to assess the variety, need, and appropriateness of subjects by asking trusted listeners what they think would help the congregation's care. Involving more people can add insight into what subjects are needed. It can also indicate those most helpful in the past. I confess that my ego and others' diplomacy (either too much or too little) make me hesitant to ask them to evaluate what I just preached. However, when I ask others

3. Timothy Keller, *Preaching: Communicating Faith in an Age of Skepticism* (New York: Viking, 2015), 39–41.

to help me plan, their insights come more naturally and without as much danger.

Listener engagement can also temper, sharpen, and expand the way preachers address subjects. Many experienced preachers advise inviting parishioners of various ages, backgrounds, and struggles to their kitchen table or coffee shop to ask for impressions about the wording or emphasis of a message. Many of my messages are quite different (improved, I pray) because I considered the responses of a wounded, resistant, or thoughtful soul.

Expand Structure Variety

Genre Sensitivity

Many years ago, I gave a series of messages on the life of David at a friend's church. When I finished, he asked, "How do you do that?" "Do what?" I asked. He continued, "How do you preach from the historical biographies of the Bible? I only preach from the Epistles of the New Testament and the Psalms of the Old Testament, because I was never taught how to preach expository sermons from Bible stories."

His words initially shocked me. Since three-quarters of the Bible is historical narrative, how could my friend exclude so much of the Bible and think he was preaching the "whole counsel of God"? I was ready to judge his shortsightedness, until I considered how teaching such as my own may have contributed to limiting the texts my friend would preach.

He had rightly been taught that an expository sermon gets its topic, main points, and subpoints from the text, but he had only been taught how to do so from didactic passages. In such passages, paragraphs of thought and theology readily divide into a logical outline of major and subordinate ideas. Such traditional exposition comes naturally to our Western linear thinking. However, my friend hadn't been prepared to see how truth principles are related through plot or character development in biblical narratives, through literary devices or image echoes in biblical poetry, through theme developments across biblical books and history, or through prophetic nuance and utterance across time and eternity.

His tools of academic outlining were a confining cookie cutter for the many varieties of biblical literature. His texts, subjects, and sermons became more varied as he learned not only to fit the biblical contents into an academic outline but also to structure his messages to reflect the development of the text. A biblical plot often moves from situation to complication to gospel resolution—with the ending frequently unexpected. A biblical character's development may move from naiveté to maturity, from godlessness to godliness, from misunderstanding to wisdom, or in the reverse order of any of these tandems. Biblical poetry may communicate truth by word repetition, literary echoes, ironic twists, or structural cues. Prophetic literature can address issues or events in the past, present, or future and can run back and forth through vast epochs.

Our goal in discerning the way each passage or genre of Scripture communicates biblical truth is to be able to proclaim, "This is the truth this passage teaches," *and*, "This is how I know the biblical writer is communicating that truth." The more our sermon structure allows the thought and structure of the text to show and have the effect the original author intended, the more variety will be in our sermons, and the more they will conform to the text's purposes.[4]

Sensitivity to the text's nature may mean that the sermon will develop more through mention of events with chronological development, through moves of plot with ironic or surprise development, or through echoes of words and threads of themes in poetic development than through traditionally worded main points. The truths of the text must eventually be made plain, but they may be stated or illustrated at the end of a section of the sermon's development (which is an inductive approach more typical of story development and ordinary conversation), rather than at the beginning

---

4. Jeffrey D. Arthurs, *Preaching with Variety: How to Re-create the Dynamics of Biblical Genres* (Grand Rapids, MI: Kregel, 2007), 16–28, 86–95.

of each main point (which is a deductive approach more suited to didactic passages and academic presentation).

Congregation Sensitivity

Once we become open to moving beyond a cookie-cutter structure for every message, we may begin to recognize why so many of our sermons sound the same even though their points and explanations vary. The traditional deductive structure lends itself to stating a problem and then identifying or proving a solution. The problem-to-solution approach appeals to the academic mind, but it sets up an unfortunate dynamic with listeners if it's a preacher's *only* style. Week-in-and-week-out declarations of "You have a problem, and I have a solution" not only can seem like the same old song but also can set up a patronizing or even antagonistic dynamic between preacher and listeners. The more time and energy the preacher spends in pressing or proving the problem each week, the likelier it is that negative dynamics will develop. Spiritual conviction is a necessary feature of biblical preaching; a steady drumbeat of pulpit condemnation is not.

We can vary overall approaches and impressions by recognizing that many texts (and the overall gospel message) are more about declaring a solution than proving a problem. We move toward a more edifying stance and more structural possibilities when we specify a problem or need that our people can identify with early in the message (usually in the introduction) and then use the bulk of the message to show how the text identifies either a plan for handling the problem or the advantages of implementing such a plan.[5] Not only do these

5. See Bryan Chapell, "Alternative Models," in *Handbook of Contemporary Preaching*, ed. Michael Duduit (Nashville: Broadman, 1992), 117–31. Tony Merida lists ten organizational patterns in *Faithful Preaching: Declaring Scripture with Responsibility, Passion, and Authenticity* (Nashville: B&H, 2009), 92–92; Barbara Tucker and Brenda Buckley Hunter list eleven organizational patterns in *Introductory Speech Communication: Overcoming Obstacles, Reaching Goals* (Dubuque, IA: Kendall-Hunt, 1988), 31–32. More possibilities abound; cf. Donald R. Sunukjian, *Invitation to Biblical Preaching: Proclaiming Truth with Clarity and Relevance*, Invitation to Theological Studies Series 2 (Grand Rapids, MI: Kregel, 2007), 27–41, 143–55; Kenton C. Anderson, *Choosing to Preach: A Comprehensive Introduction to Sermon Options and Structures* (Grand Rapids, MI: Zondervan, 2009), 65, 70, 85. Standard structural

need-plan and plan-advantage approaches add variety to our structural tool kit, they create more of a "good news" atmosphere in the sermon ecology created by the pastor. Here are four ways I'd suggest that you can be sensitive to your congregation.

Determine Significance as Well as Meaning

Commitment to communicating a text's inspired purpose requires that we determine a text's significance before preaching its content. Sadly, those who think of themselves as expositors are often experts at preaching truths without reasons. We do a data dump on our people and wonder why they appear bored or burdened. We do that because we have forgotten that we are not merely ministers of information but ministers of transformation. If the truths we declare have no apparent purpose other than to inform, then we should not be surprised that our sermons are of little interest to those whose goal is not to make a better grade on the theology test that never comes.

Preaching effectiveness grows when preachers recognize that our people don't really know the meaning of a text if they don't know its significance for their lives. Bare cognitive registration of biblical facts and theological truths is not the goal of preaching designed to enable God's people to love him with all their heart, soul, mind, and strength (Luke 10:27) so that whether they eat or drink or whatever they do, they will do all to the glory of God (1 Cor. 10:31).

Discern Burden as Well as Facts

We discern the purpose of Scripture by identifying the burden of the text before we explain the content of the text. We must not fall into what a friend calls "factoid preaching." We must determine *why* a text was written before we recite the facts it contains.

alternatives include problem to solution, proof of contention, cause to effect, effect to cause, explanation and application, story with moral, elimination of wrong alternatives (called the "chase outline" because a preacher chases down wrong leads to find a right answer), answers to a provocative question, and unfolding dimensions of a controlling image or story or biographical sequence.

If we spend the effort to ascertain the specific purpose for which the Holy Spirit inspired a particular text for fallen creatures in a fallen world, and we indicate how that purpose applies to our lives, then we'll advance that text's goals. We'll also address the longing of God's people for us to move beyond tired clichés and personal hobby horses in our sermons.

We determine the burden of the text by first determining the reason it was written to the original audience (e.g., were they sad, lonely, rebellious, fearful, doubting, distracted in worship, distant in affection, or grieving over affliction?). Then we need to identify how our people share that fallen condition (in heart or circumstance or both). We do this because Scripture itself tells us that its contents are not random or merely descriptive but are intended to be applied to our present situations (Rom. 15:4).

Once we identify that mutual fallen condition, then we're prepared to show the significance of the text to our people's lives. The more insightful and specific the preacher is about the mutual condition of the original scriptural audience and the modern-day church listeners, the more the Bible will come alive with contemporary significance. Further, the more specific and personal our focus on the fallen condition is, the more pointed and powerful our application will be.[6]

Identify Specifics as Well as Principles

It's difficult to overestimate the importance of identifying the fallen condition being addressed by the hope of the biblical text. The reason people are sitting in church is that they hope the preacher can explain how the gospel has significance for their needs and hurts. When we demonstrate that we understand that hope and that Scripture addresses it, boredom turns into anticipation, and calloused commitment to endure another sermon becomes eagerness to hear God's Word.

6. Bryan Chapell, *Christ-Centered Preaching: Redeeming the Expository Sermon*, 3rd ed. (Grand Rapids, MI: Baker Academic, 2018), 28–32.

Eagerness will wane, however, if the application remains abstract or merely theoretical. Generic applications of "go and do likewise" or "read your Bible more, pray more, and go to church more" are another cause of sermons that sound too similar to inspire. Variety worthy of the significance of our texts identifies the situations to which they apply today. This requires more than regurgitating a commentary and calling it a sermon. The text supplies the truth we are to apply, but our pastoral interaction with God's people provides the situational relevance that makes those truths real and applicable.

We shouldn't be ashamed to acknowledge that new preachers are at a disadvantage in applying texts to the struggles, pains, and challenges of messy lives that dominate congregations. Longer experience will add depth, variety, and reality to our applications. Still, we should not resign ourselves to clichéd applications at any stage of ministry. The fastest way to move sermons into the crucibles of life is first to discern the significance of the truth a biblical text teaches and then to enter congregational lives through the "who door." In your study ask, *Who needs to hear this?* Then in the sermon, do not identify those people, but identify their situations as addressed by this passage.[7]

This approach not only keeps sermons from ending with legalistic lists (mis)labeled as application but also actually enables people

7. See Chapell, *Christ-Centered Preaching*, 196, to identify how the following categories of common concern can help preachers consider situational specifics in their congregation that need application of the principles in a text:

- Building proper relationships (with God, family, friends, coworkers, church people, etc.)
- Reconciling conflicts (in marriage, family, work, church, etc.)
- Handling difficult situations (stress, debt, unemployment, grief, fatigue, etc.)
- Overcoming weakness and sin (dishonesty, anger, addiction, lust, doubt, lack of discipline, etc.)
- Lacking or improperly using resources (time, treasures, talents, etc.)
- Meeting challenges and using opportunities (education, work in or out of church, witnessing, missions, etc.)
- Taking responsibility (home, church, work, finances, future, etc.)
- Honoring God (worship, confession, prayer, devotions, not compartmentalizing life, etc.)
- Addressing social or world problems (poverty, racism, abortion, education, injustice, war, creation, etc.)

to see how Scripture applies to their situations and demonstrates how it helps them in their difficulties. Then we truly shepherd people in our sermons, rather than burdening them with greater loads of performance-driven duties.

Preach the Fullness of the Gospel

Burdens will remain, however, if we don't demonstrate from the text how God enables his people to know his love and to do what he requires. The antidote to tired legalisms is not weekly repetition of "This is what God requires, but you can't do it, so trust his grace of forgiveness." The gospel is more than a message of forgiveness; it's the promise that "greater is he that is in you, than he that is in the world" (1 John 4:4 KJV). We must be clear that the grace pervading all Scripture culminates in the Christ who now indwells his people to ignite love for him and to enable their victories over sin (John 14:4–6; Rom. 6:6, 14; 2 Cor. 4:14). Complaints that gospel-centered preaching is the same every week are only true when preachers have not discovered the varieties of ways God provides for people who cannot provide for themselves to enable their victories over the world, the flesh, and the devil.[8]

Few critics of Christ-centered messages say, "Every week I preach the same message: law, law, law." They recognize that there are too many aspects of the law of God for such a charge to stand. Sadly, they fail to see that the grace of God is as rich and varied. If we will take care to disclose the specific burden of each biblical text we preach and the specific aspect of grace that relieves that burden, then we will preach with the variety and power that the gospel of God intends.

Be encouraged, dear brother. Ask God to give you an awareness that the mercies of his Word are new each day (and each week) for both you and your congregation.

---

8. Keller, *Preaching*, 20–22, 56–69.

4

I'm under the Fire of Criticism

Dan Doriani

Dear Pastor Dan,

I know you've had long seasons of peace in your years of ministry, but I know you've endured strong criticism too. I realize that criticism can be friendly, so that it feels like a little rain at a picnic. But it can also strike like a tsunami that threatens to drown its victims. For the last month, I've felt the tsunami.

Let me explain, and I'll leave out names to protect the guilty.

Last week, a church member visited my office and informed me that she had been keeping a close watch on both my life and my doctrine. As to my life, she complained that I talk too much, that I preach too long, and that my attention span is too short—especially when she's trying to talk to me. As to my doctrine, this loquacious lady went on to call me a Presbyterian in Baptist clothing because in our study of Ephesians, I dared discuss the doctrines of predestination and election the first week. Never mind that these topics dominate the early words of this powerful epistle. Further, this sister informed me that her family was leaving our church for a larger one across town, one with a hyperactive youth group.

The next day, a deacon stopped by and wanted to know why he never sees my vehicle parked in front of the church (I tend to park in the back), especially at a few minutes after 5 p.m. Before departing, he called me "lazy" but also a "typical pastor." Yesterday, two of my elders met with me and ticked off several pages from a list of things I've been doing wrong as pastor over the last few months, including too much talk about evangelism, too little visiting of our shut-ins, too much time in sermon preparation and prayer (the authenticity of which they questioned), and too much time at my son's baseball games.

Today, our financial secretary let me know that the church's general account is operating at quite a deficit and suspects our people are failing to tithe out of rebellion against me. His counsel was to begin preaching topical sermons with less emphasis on doctrine and more emphasis on homespun stories. Doctrine is for the seminary, stories are for the people, he said, subtly hinting that I'd perhaps be happier as a professor than as a pastor.

Of my several years at this church, heated criticism has been fairly constant and has come from various corners. To be frank, this week may be the final straw for my ministry here. I don't know if pastoral ministry is for me, and I'm growing in certainty that this church with all its critics is not my future. Please tell me what you think. Is it always going to be this way? Am I justified in shaking the dust from my feet in the face of such treatment? Surely this isn't normative.

Faithfully yours,

Pastor in the Flames

Dear Pastor in the Flames,[1]

Criticism is a universal element of leadership, and church leaders are not exempt. Most pastors hear far more praise than blame, but complaints feel bad more than compliments feel good, and they stick in the memory. A renowned pastor, who was both a great preacher and a visionary leader, endured such criticism from his church that he almost despaired. He told a confidant, "After twelve years as a pastor, I had to put a wall between myself and my people so I wouldn't have to quit the ministry."[2]

To understand criticism, you must first grasp that it is inevitable. Even the most talented, fruitful, and godly pastors feel the lash. Consider three gifted lead pastors:

- Mike is an introvert. That lets him sit and craft insightful sermons in which he makes great points in sparkling language, but the introversion that permits him to sit and think also makes him a social disappointment to his detractors.
- Bill is a strong preacher whose sterling organizational skills let him direct growing ministries locally and internationally. But he works at such a pace that critics say he never has time for his people.
- Jack is also a fine preacher. Supremely friendly, he *always* has time for his people, yet his elders say he ignores leadership duties.

Looking for a Few Perfect Men

Some of the greatest pastors were fired because of their flaws. John Calvin's unbending zeal and refusal to compromise led Geneva to expel him after two years (they recalled him three years later). Jonathan Edwards's Northampton church dismissed him after

1. Portions of this chapter are adapted from Dan Doriani, "Why Do Churches Wound Their Pastors," The Gospel Coalition, May 23, 2017, https://www.thegospelcoalition.org/article/why-do-churches-wound-their-pastors/. Used by permission of the author.

2. Every illustration in this chapter rests on real events, but I altered details and created composite characters to protect confidentiality. If you read an anecdote and think "I know *exactly* who that is," you have erred.

twenty-three years following a series of missteps and a failure to navigate the town's complicated political waters. Edwards had a hard time listening to his critics.

My work often leads me to visit larger churches as they search for a new pastor. When I meet with the search team, I notice that (1) they want their next lead pastor to be virtually perfect, and (2) they hope to fix the weakness they perceived in their previous pastor. Churches looking to replace Mike and Bill (p. 43) will want a pastor to be *more* sociable. Churches led by Jack will want one to be *less* so. (3) By contrast, churches *occasionally* want a new pastor to be exactly like the previous man, especially beloved founding pastors or those who died in office. This leads to the "unintended interim" effect.[3]

Imagine that Jack recently retired, and I consult with his church's search committee. I'll tell them two things. First, look for character, work ethic, and the gifts your church most needs. Don't look for the perfect pastor; his name is Jesus, he isn't available, and remember, they killed him. Second, don't look for a senior pastor who's just like Jack but without his "fatal flaw." Every pastor has an apparently fatal flaw. If you solve Jack's alleged disinterest in organization, you will get someone who is a weaker preacher or less pastoral, because no one is equally good at everything. Address his weaknesses by hiring the right support staff. Hiring a complementary pastor also makes it clear that the lead pastor can't do everything or care for everyone.

Naturally, churches want ideal pastors. But criticism of the *best* senior leaders shows that everyone is susceptible, since no one has every gift. Even if someone did, he would seem to fail, because his time would be limited. Lead pastors and high-energy associate pastors face daunting schedules. Because they can't always socialize, they seem abrupt. This is unavoidable, yet it offends. Yes, the ideal pastor will be equally adept at preaching and teaching, casting

3. I owe this point to Scott Sauls, a wise lead pastor and friend.

vision and leading, counseling and mentoring. But no human *excels* at every task.

If Jack's church found a pastor bent on leadership, he would inevitably be less devoted to preaching or shepherding. No one has the time to be a strong preacher, organizer, and shepherd even if he has all three abilities.

So, friend, if you struggle with fiery criticism, join the team. I once asked a group of church leaders to name their greatest problem. They replied, "Opposition from subversive coleaders and self-appointed critics within the church." Let's consider why this is true, how to appraise the main types of criticism, and how to respond to them with biblical wisdom. For our discussion, we can place criticism in three categories: the deserved, the inevitable, and the undeserved.

Fair Criticism

We all *deserve* criticism. Pastors are sinners too. We sin in private and at work. When exhausted, we get irritable; when thwarted, we become angry; and when self-discipline wanes, we prepare insufficiently for our duties. We speak without preparing adequately. We lead meetings without creating an agenda or framing the issues well. As counselors, we listen poorly, thinking, *Can you please get to the point?* and people feel our impatience.

Good churches love their pastors but also see their weaknesses. At best, they state necessary corrections gently, with encouragement and concrete suggestions for improvement. The solo pastor of a small church once told me, "At one point, I really thought that if I preached good sermons, everything else would take care of itself." His people rightly objected to his habit of hiding in his office and told him to get out more. He resisted briefly, then listened to people who had a proper interest in their pastor's growth.

Correction can be gentle or severe, and because it's easier to hear gentle correction than fiery criticism (2 Tim. 2:25), a wise pastor will invite trusted friends and colaborers to come to him with their concerns about his leadership. Still, regardless of the critics' presentation, we should listen.

In an important sense, critics can't hurt us. Our friends and fellow workers speak in love—they want us to become the best version of ourselves. If they're right, even with flawed motives, they give us opportunity to correct a mistake or address a weakness. If they're wrong, the Lord knows. Normally, there is at least partial truth to a charge. After all, critics look for flaws. Sometimes it's best *not* to consider the source and instead to listen, taking all plausible criticism seriously. Regardless of the motive (Phil. 1:15–18), we seize every opportunity to grow. We examine ourselves and ask others to evaluate us. To discern your flaws, consult your supervisor, lean on wise pastors and mentors, and confide in loyal peers.

It might seem as if there are only two kinds of criticism, accurate and inaccurate, fair and unfair, but there is another category, criticism that is both or neither—criticism that arises from the structures of life.

Inevitable Criticism: Neither Fair nor Unfair

A certain amount of disagreement, disappointment, and at least apparent criticism seems fundamental to postfall society. The reasons are several. First, a pastor with any call to leadership inevitably collaborates with talented, successful, and opinionated people who love him but disagree with his perspective on positions from time to time.

Second, if the pastor hears but ultimately rejects a volunteer's counsel or proposal, that volunteer will be disappointed and may say so loudly, especially if the pastor's plan doesn't work well. This is inevitable.

Third, pastors see problems that invite, even demand, reform. Most people resist change. Those who are committed to the existing order will resist proposals for a new system. It's wise to move slowly on major changes, to build consensus, but the day of decision will come. Everyone who has thrived under the old system is an enemy, and those who *may* thrive in the new order will be lukewarm allies.

Even if change is effective and the church grows, another problem arises. Dynamic leaders always face opposition. A rapidly growing urban church will rouse protests from its neighbors over increased noise and traffic. Nearby pastors, possibly jealous, will imagine that they detect compromise, even heterodoxy. Heroes like Anselm, John Chrysostom, Martin Luther, John Calvin, John Wesley, and Jonathan Edwards tasted fierce resistance. Because they addressed burning theological debates, confrontation was certain. Anyone with skill and influence becomes a target—even young pastors.

Finally, pastors will suffer criticism for errors by their team members. If a volunteer misbehaves, the pastor failed at oversight. If a staff member or pastor commits a major sin, who hired this person? Who failed to correct a problem in its early stages? Didn't the pastor see the way the assistant pastor hugged women? Didn't he see that the youth leader was wobbly at the staff party? On the one hand, pastors are certainly responsible for exercising due diligence in hiring and in oversight of staff. But on the other hand, this criticism is often unfair, since no pastor is omniscient and since people are quite adept at hiding their sins. This takes us to patently unjust criticism.

Unwarranted Criticism

Cruelty and criticism have always been problems, but cultural trends exacerbate the situation. Consumerism leads many to view the church as a provider of spiritual services, and if worship or the youth program doesn't satisfy them, they say so—loudly. Americans can't bear disappointment in silence, and all too often church members behave more like Americans than disciples of Jesus. They think of church membership as a contract for services rather than a covenant between God and his people. Further, the rules of social media now permit coarse discourse, a sense that one can say anything, anonymously, without consequences. Everyone is a potential critic, even if he or she knows nothing about the topic.

By God's grace, I eventually became friendly with an older woman who initially avoided me. One day we were talking in the kitchen, and she confessed, "When I joined this church three years ago, I hated you. I don't know why. I didn't even know you, but I hated you." Irrational anger rarely ends so well.

A man once walked into my office and shouted wild accusations at me for ten or fifteen minutes. Eventually, he paused momentarily, and I told him, in a barely elevated voice, "You need to stop shouting." He then left my office and told people I had pounded my desk, yelled at him, and kicked him out of my office for no reason. Because he was active in the church, a few believed him, especially those who shared his views on liturgy. These vignettes allow to me offer a rough typology of critics. Here are five:

1. True friends offer constructive criticism and present it in ways we readily hear, because they love us and God's church.
2. Ministry allies make the same points for the sake of kingdom work but perhaps state them harshly.[4]
3. Jealousy, love of power, or great disappointment can lead to chronic suspicion.
4. Strong, systemic differences of opinion or a low view of another person's skill or self-discipline can lead to significant clashes. At worst, critics interpret the pastor's actions in the worst possible way, escalating even minor problems.
5. Full-blown antagonists, the burn-it-all-down types, make concerted attacks, without factual basis, to drive pastors away or destroy them. It's possible that for all their religion, they serve the evil one. There is a religion that leads one away from God, as Jesus's opponents show. Satan is the ultimate critic, the "accuser of the brethren," and he exploits human weakness and weaponizes human anger.

4. On insensitivity, a remarkable number of pastors report that their leaders joke about cutting their salaries or benefits or firing them.

False Accusations

How then shall we respond to false accusations? First, remember that strong leaders always face opposition. Remember Moses, David, Elijah, Isaiah, Jeremiah, Jesus, Peter, and Paul. They challenged the status quo, and they aroused envy (e.g., Num. 12:1–8).

Second, when you are falsely accused, remember that the Lord knows the truth and that most people do too. Further, we all have sins that go undetected. We are criminals who are falsely accused of one crime but erroneously unindicted for ten others.

Third, preposterous accusations can reveal more about the accuser than the accused. Certainly, some people are able to discern when others are lying or acting from ill motives. But in some cases, liars shout, "That's a lie"; conspirators cry, "It's a conspiracy"; and the greedy assume, "He's only in it for the money."

Fourth, ask the Lord for discernment. There's a time to defend our reputation, for "a good name is [better] than great riches" (Prov. 22:1). Yet fools love to quarrel (Prov. 20:3; 26:4–5), and there's a time to forgo self-defense. Some accusers won't listen, and certain judges care nothing for justice, as Jesus well knew (Matt. 26:62; 27:12–14). When speech is pointless, it's wise to keep silent.

Finally, seek to hold two truths in creative tension: (1) no one has every skill, and yet (2) a weakness is still a weakness, and we should try to remedy major deficits. Israel had three regular offices—prophet, priest, and king—and none but Jesus held all three (only Melchizedek, Moses, and perhaps David held two). No one is equally gifted as prophet, teaching and preaching; as king, leading and organizing; and as priest, praying and caring. That's why God gave the church a plurality of leaders.

Right Response

The right ways to respond to critics are generally clear. First, let's remember that we've received God's unconditional love by faith and enjoy status as his children. God knows our worst sins and forgives them. That counts vastly more than any man's condemnation.

While people always want their pastors to do more and are disappointed if they don't, Jesus has already done everything for us, and nothing we do can make him love us more or be more pleased with us. That's an encouraging thought.

Second, focus on the good the Lord does through you. No decision, no style of evangelism, discipleship, or teaching pleases everyone. If 75–80 percent of the people are behind you and another 10–15 percent respect you, give thanks.

Third, examine yourself. List the criticisms you hear. Which are mostly true? Partly true? Wholly false? Forget the falsehood, and work on the others, especially the weightier ones. Ask yourself, *Which criticisms bother me more than they should? Why is that so?* Then preach the gospel to yourself: "If God is for us, who can be against us? . . . It is God who justifies. Who is to condemn?" (Rom. 8:31, 33–34). Yes, humans condemn, but who are they, compared to the Lord who loves and justifies? Since we are secure in God's love, it's possible (though difficult) for us to love our critics. After all, Jesus said, "Love your enemies, do good to those who hate you, bless those who curse you, pray for those who abuse you" (Luke 6:27–28). We still have a right to protect ourselves and our reputation, but we should call down grace, not fire. That response demonstrates our trust in Jesus and his gospel.[5]

Finally, when the self-examination is complete, find your spouse, friends, and mentors. Leadership is not an individual sport. The Lord loves you, and he will show that through true friends.

5. I owe this point to Scotty Smith, a wise pastor and friend.

5

I Would Never Have Attended the Church I Now Lead

Tom Ascol

Dear Pastor Tom,

I am a few months into my pastorate here, and I have come to feel as much like a circus leader as a pastor. To illustrate, I'll begin with our hymnody. Last month, our music minister asked if he could Christianize Bette Midler's song "From a Distance" and use it in corporate worship. A similar level of madness has also infected our evangelism; a group of ladies recently asked if they could take their clown ministry (no, your eyes are not deceiving you) to the local strip mall on Saturday and seek to win the lost to Jesus on behalf of our church. They sent me an email hoping the "new pastor" would "get fully behind" their evangelistic ministry, adding an attachment with a flyer touting our church as "the church of clowns." The irony's too obvious there to warrant further comment. I think their desire to win the lost to Jesus is absolutely commendable, but . . .

That's not all. Our Wednesday night children's teacher has written a song that includes lyrics that are not only biblically questionable but also borderline bawdy (if I understand them accurately). The teacher of the senior adult men has informed me that he would like to begin a series of studies that bypasses the Bible and instead exegetes the *Left Behind* books and video series. I half jokingly asked him if they'd like to include the *Left Behind* board game in their studies, to which he replied (with a straight face that told me he completely overlooked the tongue in my cheek), "We shouldn't play games in church, pastor. We need to stick to teaching from the Bible."

I could go on and on, but I'll stop with those windows into the soul of the church I inherited. This congregation needs serious revitalization—the sooner, the better. Though I know what I should do, I'm not sure how quickly I should do it. I realize the people need to get to know me better before they'll truly follow me, so making wholesale (but necessary) changes impatiently seems dangerous both for my ministry and for the church itself. How can I make changes without sinking the ship? How can I lead them in the right direction while showing church members the grace and respect that is surely due to Christ's people?

When have I established enough credibility to change the big things, and how long should I wait to work on the small things? For example, the New Testament teaches that a church is best led by plural leadership. When should I go to work on that transition? It seems that that may require a season of in-depth teaching wedded with patience—more of a long-view thing. But the Bette Midler music—shouldn't that be scuttled immediately? If not, can a sanctified rendition of "Stairway to Heaven" be far behind? Several people love that particular feature of our church's worship—seriously.

Honestly, I'd never join this church, and if I were a visitor, I'd run far and fast. Help me! I'm anxious to show the church a more excellent way but need profound guidance as to how and when it's wise to move things in a more biblical, Christ-centered direction.

Grace and peace,

Bewildered Young Pastor

Dear Bewildered Young Pastor,

I laughed out loud when I read your letter—not because there is anything funny in what you are facing but because it all sounds so familiar. The church that I have been serving for more than thirty-two years sounds a lot like the one you are now pastoring.

Looking back, I can honestly say that I never would have joined Grace Baptist Church if the Lord had not called me to pastor here. However, I can also say that I am glad he did call me here, because over the last three decades, I have been given a front row seat to his steadfast love and the power of his Word in the life of a local church.

I first heard about Grace a few weeks after I resigned from a church I had served for five years. Because of a combination of trials stemming from that experience and my ongoing graduate studies, I was discouraged and increasingly doubtful of any future usefulness in ministry. Grace Baptist was young—only three years old—and had fired their founding pastor while he was on vacation. Several candidates had already turned them down, and they were getting desperate.

They were a church nobody wanted, and I was a pastor nobody wanted. It was a match made in heaven. I was finishing up PhD seminars and preparing for a comprehensive oral examination when I accepted the call. On a quick trip from north Texas to south Florida, we formalized our agreement, and I signed to purchase a house. Six weeks later, Donna and I packed up our apartment and loaded our two-year-old and six-month-old daughters into our Ford Escort to begin our move.

A few weeks after I accepted the call, before I actually started driving to Florida, the church's most influential member decided he no longer wanted me to be his pastor. He had "figured out" that I was one of those dreaded Calvinists who believes that repentance as well as faith is a required response to the gospel. He started a petition to rescind my call and intended to meet me with it upon my arrival. By God's grace, he could not get enough signatures to carry out his plan.

Needless to say, the honeymoon ended before it began, and there were tension and turmoil in the church from day one. I decided not to take a vacation for a few years. God used that early, intense difficulty (which continued in various forms for more than five years) to teach me much about my own heart and about pastoral ministry.

Today, by God's grace, the church is a loving, joyful, hope-filled congregation that readily receives teaching from God's Word and engages in a variety of significant ministries. Of course, that's not to say we are problem-free. Like all other churches, our members are Christians who still must deal with the sin in their hearts. That's true of our pastors as well. Nevertheless, the church today is as healthy as it has ever been before.

Though I don't believe that there is one definitive prescription to lead a troubled church toward greater spiritual health, there are some principles that every pastor should keep in mind as he seeks to lead a church. I wish I could say that I have never violated these at any point, but that would be far from the truth. What I can say is that they have survived the test of time and have served me well when observed.

Deal with Your Own Heart

The first and most important principle is what Charles Spurgeon calls "the minister's self-watch" (the title of the first chapter in his *Lectures to My Students*, which I highly recommend):

> Regularly apply the gospel to your own heart. As pastors, all of our gospel ministry should arise out of a deep awareness that we desperately need all that we commend to others. Do we want our people to know and love Christ supremely? And to love others sincerely? We need the same. We are dependent on God's grace and mercy every day just as our people are. We need to grow in humility and forgiveness just as they do.[1]

1. Charles H. Spurgeon, *Lectures to My Students* (Edinburgh: Banner of Truth, 2008), 1.

The Puritan pastor John Flavel said that "a crucified stile [*sic*] best suits the preachers of a crucified Christ."[2] Your people will more readily receive your teaching if they believe that you also are heeding it. Our Lord was patient and gentle with his disciples while he walked the earth. He still is. So should his ministers be.

Be Honest

A second principle grows out of the first: be honest. Don't be duplicitous or deceitful in any way. This should be a pastor's policy from the outset of his relationship to a church. I highly recommend letting the church know your core convictions about the nature and teaching of Scripture. To be transparent about my own beliefs, I gave a copy of the 1689 Second London Baptist Confession of Faith to every deacon during the candidating process when I was considering a call to Grace.

I also called particular attention to my convictions about regenerate church membership, congregational polity, elder leadership, and corrective church discipline. Those were key areas that, though the church had partially acknowledged in their written documents, they hadn't actually practiced. It's important to let the congregation know where you intend to lead them because of your biblical convictions.

Let me quickly add that I do not mean that you should spell out all your plans and convictions in detail at the outset. It's not being dishonest if you don't say everything that you think. In fact, it is the better part of wisdom not to do so. As I explain about preaching below, sometimes people aren't in a position to understand everything that could be said about a subject. Jesus told his disciples, "I still have many things to say to you, but you cannot bear them now" (John 16:12). Pastors should follow his example when gauging what and how much to say to the people under their care.

2. John Flavel, *The Works of John Flavel* (Edinburgh: Banner of Truth, 1982), 6:572.

Preach and Pray

Commit yourself early to the priorities of preaching and prayer. This is what we see the apostles doing as they lead the church in Jerusalem in Acts 6:2–4. These two priorities correspond to the provisions God has given us in his Word and Spirit. Any lasting work done in a church is done by Christ, who himself has promised to build his church such that "the gates of hell shall not prevail against it" (Matt. 16:18). Therefore, we must pray and ask him to do that as his Word is taught.

Preaching should be your most important public task. Other responsibilities are important too—such as counseling, discipling, personal evangelism, administration, and so on—but none of these should surpass preaching in your priorities. Through the week-by-week ministry of the Word, the Lord builds his church. Expositional preaching should be the staple of your pulpit ministry. Work your way through books of the Bible, prayerfully seeking guidance about which books or sections to preach at what times.

I've been greatly helped by the Westminster Larger Catechism at this point. Question 159 asks, "How is the Word of God to be preached by those that are called thereunto?" The answer is full of wisdom:

> They that are called to labor in the ministry of the word, are to preach sound doctrine, diligently, in season and out of season; plainly, not in the enticing words of man's wisdom, but in demonstration of the Spirit, and of power; faithfully, making known the whole counsel of God; wisely, applying themselves to the necessities and capacities of the hearers; zealously, with fervent love to God and the souls of his people; sincerely, aiming at his glory, and their conversion, edification, and salvation.

I'd particularly call to your attention that phrase "the necessities and capacities of the hearers." When planning what to preach, pastors should not only ask, What do the people need? but also, What can they handle?

One thing every church needs is a steady diet of expositional preaching. It may be that you will have to help them cultivate an appetite for the Word, which they will acquire as they come to understand Scripture better. You can facilitate that, with the help of God's Spirit, by working hard at simply explaining, appropriately illustrating, and carefully applying the texts that you preach. I also encourage you to include public Scripture reading in all the worship services. Learn to read the text well. Practice it. By doing so, you'll help your people learn to read and understand the Bible for themselves.

The Psalms are particularly well suited for reading aloud in worship. Of course, don't start with Psalm 119. While they may need the wonderful celebration of God's Word in that psalm, they probably won't have the capacity for it. So start with shorter psalms or small sections of Scripture, and help your people learn to appreciate hearing God's Word read.

Plan your preaching. Consider preaching through the Sermon on the Mount or 1 John, followed by Ephesians or Colossians, early in your ministry. This will allow you to teach on what a true Christian is and what the gospel is. During the first few years at Grace, I used the Sunday evening worship times to preach on various Bible doctrines, starting with the doctrine of Scripture, then God, mankind, Christ, the Holy Spirit, salvation, the Christian life, and the church. If the church doesn't regularly meet on Sunday nights, consider beginning such a service, or use a midweek night to teach systematically on Bible doctrines. You might also consider allowing for questions after each teaching, so you can clear up misconceptions and learn how people are processing your messages.

As a supplement to your preaching, you should consider starting a special study for men. Read a book with them and make it something manageable and spiritually beneficial, like *The Attributes of God* by A. W. Pink or *The Pursuit of Holiness* by Jerry Bridges. Not only will you be discipling them, you will also be teaching them to read and appreciate good books. By engaging men more informally and directly, you'll be able to recognize those who show greater potential for leadership. That, in turn, will allow you to begin further equipping them to help lead in the church.

Regarding prayer, develop the discipline of starting the day meditating on and praying through Scripture for your own benefit. Keep a journal of specific matters for which you pray. You will be humbled, challenged, and encouraged by reflecting on how you have prayed and how God has answered when you look back. Be quick to pray with and for church members.

Make a regular practice of praying through the church membership by name. I keep a membership list in my Bible for that purpose. Encourage all the members to pray for one another in this way. In addition to that, find a way to regularly contact members individually to ask them how you can pray for them. Our elders send an email to a select number of members asking how we can pray for them in our next elder meeting. By doing this, we are able to pray for specific needs of each member every few months. God hears and answers those prayers, and God's people are encouraged to know that their pastors are praying for them.

Avoid Battles

In the first few years, you will find multiple problems in the church that need your attention. Some practices will need to be changed. Some approaches to ministry and ways of thinking will need to be changed. With every need to make adjustments, you will find opportunities for conflict to erupt. Learning which battles to fight and when to fight them requires wisdom.

As a general principle, try to avoid as many battles as you can (such as changing some customs or expectations that don't directly impinge on the worship or witness of the church, like how the pastor should dress), but don't run from the ones that really matter (such as the content and nature of the preaching ministry).

Make Membership Meaningful

One of the most significant goals you should have from the outset of your ministry is to make church membership meaningful. It's likely that you'll find the number of names on the membership roll to be three to four times greater than those who actually show up for worship in any given month. Yet those absentee members have the same rights and privileges as the active members. Their votes count just as much as the votes of the members who show up, give, and serve. This is a formula for disaster. All it takes is for a few disgruntled members to decide they want the church to take an action (fire the pastor, for example) or refuse to make an important course correction (welcome Christians of other ethnicities into membership, for example) and to enlist a number of inactive members in the effort. If successful, when the vote comes, you will have the opportunity to meet numerous members whom you have never seen before but who come to "protect their church." And their votes will count just as much as anyone else's.

So teach on meaningful membership. From the outset, try to ensure that those who are recommended to the church as prospective new members have a clear testimony of conversion. Help those who are active see how important it is for the sake of protecting the gospel and the honor of Christ to have the membership roll actually approximate the actual membership participation in the life of the church. Be patient as you help people understand the nature of a local church and the necessity of following Christ as a faithful member of a church.

As the congregation comes to understand this, lead them to reach out to those inactive members who are still on the rolls in order to encourage them to return to genuine participation in the life of the church. You will probably find some who have moved away or cannot be located. Others may not want to become active in the church. Don't be surprised if a few of them are deceased. Lead the church formally to remove those who are unrecoverable.

As the membership roll increasingly comprises only active members, you'll find the church's culture changing in healthy ways. There'll be greater love within the body, a greater desire for God's Word, and a greater willingness to follow the teachings of Scripture.

Love above All

Paul writes in Colossians 3:14, "And above all these put on love, which binds everything together in perfect harmony." That's a perfect watchword for every pastor, especially for one beginning in local church ministry. Love the people the Lord has given you to shepherd. Take a sincere interest in their lives. You'll discover that your expressed love for them will cause them to trust and follow your leadership more than anything else you do.

Pastoring a church is a high calling. Pastoring a disorderly, needy church can make that calling especially challenging. By God's grace, as you embrace the challenge, you will put the power of the gospel on display. Through the gospel, the lost will be converted, the church will be strengthened, and most importantly, God will be glorified.

6

My Critics Are a Burden for My Wife

Juan R. Sanchez with Jeanine D. Sanchez

Dear Pastor Juan,

It would delight my soul to be able to write you from a better frame of mind and report the great things the Lord is doing here in our local body. Regretfully, the waters of ministry have again grown tumultuous here these past two years. Two of my elders seem determined to make war with each other, and the temperature has risen between them to a point that their wives are no longer speaking. Also, I have a sneaking feeling that each man has drawn a faction within the church to himself, and both groups are calling for my ouster.

This situation is keeping me awake at night and has me crying out to God in the manner of David, "How long, O Lord?" But here's the worst part: my beloved wife is feeling the blows I'm absorbing. She hears the whispers about my leadership, she sees the cold glares from the angry elders (and their wives), and she's even heard numerous questions regarding my integrity. All this is exacting an awful toll on her.

Because of her deep love for me, I fear she will grow bitter toward our members, bitter toward the ministry, and worse, bitter toward the church. If she's not kept from it by God's grace, it's easy to see how that might happen. Right now, I know she is bedeviled by the twin demons of anger and resentment.

I am desperate for your wisdom. How can I serve as a beacon to guide her heart safely ashore through such treacherous waters? How can I help her resist the temptations to anger, resentment, and bitterness? How can I help keep her eyes riveted on the Savior when surely her flesh is whispering, "Vengeance is mine"? I want this to be an occasion of maturity, growth, and strengthening for her. To paraphrase Paul, wretched man that I am, who will deliver her from this flirtation with death?

Please send along your counsel with great haste.

Faithfully your son in Christ,

Feeling Battered and Bruised

Dear Feeling Battered and Bruised,

To say the least, my wife and I have walked a mile in your shoes. Let me start here: "We outlast all our pastors; we'll outlast you too." That's what a church member shared with my wife one Sunday morning in a soft, calm, matter-of-fact voice. She was right. I lasted only four and a half years.

It was my first pastorate. I went in committed to being at this small rural church for the rest of my vocational ministry. But there was no honeymoon. Conflict began almost immediately. As is usually the case, the "dissenters" were small in number, but they made a lot of noise. Soon, the older couple who had welcomed us so lovingly turned on us and left the church. The deacon's wife who taught our children in Sunday school refused to look at my wife when she dropped off our girls. And as the lone pastor, I had no one to confide in—no one, that is, except my wife. She was always by my side, always encouraging me, always listening. But though she may disagree, there were times when I shared with her too often, leaned on her too hard, and expected of her too much.

Oddly, we saw encouraging fruit during this difficult season of ministry, but the cloud remained: questions regarding my leadership, criticisms concerning my preaching, suspicions about my motives. After four and a half years of seemingly continuous conflict, it became clear that I was unable to help this congregation. Our desires for ministry were different; our views of the church were different; our expectations of one another were different. They were frustrated; I was frustrated. The only merciful thing for me to do was leave so that they might call a pastor they could follow. I resigned immediately with nowhere to go and no church to serve.

As I look back on that first pastorate, I thank God for it. It was my "humbling." God showed me that ministry must be done in his strength, not mine. It was my "crucible." God allowed me to go through the fire of suffering to mold me into the pastor I am today. It was my "testing." God confirmed my calling to pastoral ministry in the heat of the battle. And through it all, there was Jeanine. She was always for me, never against me. But God taught me that while she is always in my corner, she is never to be in the ring.

Marital Foundation

Ironically, my relationship with Jeanine began much like my first pastorate. After an idealistic start, we quickly experienced conflict—lots of conflict! Wisely, Jeanine's mom intervened and called her pastor. He walked us through eight weeks of premarital counseling. It was the best thing that happened to us. Like that first church, she and I had different desires, different goals, and different expectations. But throughout counseling, God knit our hearts together.

I learned to love my future wife as God made her, and I was prepared to live with her "according to knowledge"—the knowledge I obtained throughout the premarital process (1 Pet. 3:7 KJV).

If we are to live with our wife "according to knowledge," we must become students, majoring in the subject of "her." Though men and women are created equal as image bearers, God designed us men to lead, protect, and provide for our families, and he designed our wives to follow our leadership, seek our protection, and welcome our provision. But we not only need to learn how God created women in general, we each also need to learn how God created our own woman in particular.

Your wife isn't just like any other woman. Do you know her strengths and weaknesses, her fears and concerns? Do you understand what builds her up, what tears her down, what encourages and discourages her? Are you aware of which stressors she can process healthily and which ones overwhelm her? Living with your wife according to knowledge is a lifelong learning process that requires diligence. Don't be passive. It's hard work that takes continuous, intentional effort.

Mercifully, marital love is grounded in God and the gift of his Son. It's empowered by the Holy Spirit. And it's lived out on the basis of his Word. If you want your wife to grow and blossom under your care, you must build your marriage on this foundation. If your wife is wilting and fading, it's your responsibility to learn what she needs so that you may know how to help her. Brothers, let's give ourselves to loving our wives in such a way that they may thrive under our care and in our ministries.

Always in Your Corner

As you lead your family at home and your wife flourishes, she, too, will learn how to help and encourage you (you'll need to help her know how to do this). She will seek to use words that build you up and avoid those that tear you down. Because she is your helper, your wife will point out your weaknesses and, in love, confront you when you sin. She will cheer you on as you pursue your dreams and stand up for you when others dash your hopes.

Because you two are one, she'll feel your pain and share your sorrows. And when church conflict comes, because she is in your corner, she'll be tempted to get in the ring and fight your fight. That's when you must remind her that she is not to get in the ring. You are the pastor; she is not. You are the recognized authority in the church; she is not. You are fully informed; she is not. And remind her also that even though it may be hard for her to sit by and watch from outside the ring, it's for her blessing and protection.

Her Roles

Your wife's primary role is to be your helper. This may sound obvious, but you need to continually remind your wife, your children, and your church that God's design for marriage applies to you as well. A godly wife is an amazing helper. Of course she'll help you in ministry, but first and foremost, she must help you be a man of God, a faithful husband, and if the Lord has given you children, an intentional father. Too many churches think that when they call a married pastor, they're getting a "two for one" deal. Sadly, some pastors (and some pastors' wives) fall for this "bargain" arrangement.

Your wife's secondary role is to be a mother. If the Lord has blessed you with children, you and your wife have a responsibility to raise them "in the discipline and instruction of the Lord" (Eph. 6:4). Because the church has called you, your wife serves an important role in freeing you to be a faithful shepherd of the flock and an engaged father at home. She will help protect you from sacrificing your family on the altar of ministry.

Of course, your wife is also to be a good church member. Whatever you expect of church members, you can expect of her. It's important to communicate this fact to the church from the beginning (and regularly afterward). To ward off expectations that your wife will be the pianist, the children's minister, or the women's Bible study leader, you need to let the church know up front that your wife's priorities are to be your helper and the mother of your children. And yet, even with the priority of those roles, she still needs to be a faithful church member. That will require sacrifice on her (and your) part but no more than what you would expect of any other church family member.

That your wife is just another faithful church member also means that she needs discipleship relationships within the church. She needs to serve other ladies, and she needs other ladies to lead and serve her. And like other church members, she also needs friends—friends to have fun with, friends to laugh with, and friends to cry with. Be willing to make the necessary sacrifices to free her to pursue and develop such friendships. Also, so your wife may experience some much-needed time alone, spend time with your children. That's called parenting, not babysitting.

In the Heat of the Battle

Still, because all Christians are growing in the grace and knowledge of Christ in varying degrees of maturity, there will be church conflict. Pastors are often the focus of regular criticism and even personal attacks. So you and your wife will need to learn how to face conflict. Here are some lessons Jeanine and I learned from my first pastorate.

Pursue Christ and Picture the Gospel

It's no accident that the Bible begins (Gen. 2:18–25) and ends with a marriage (Rev. 19:6–9). And in Ephesians 5:31–32, the apostle Paul reminds us that in the first marriage, God already had the last one in mind. Earthly marriage is to picture the gospel—Christ's pursuit of his bride "that he might sanctify her, having cleansed her by the washing of water with the word, so that he might present the church to himself in splendor, without spot or wrinkle or any such thing, that she might be holy and without blemish" (Eph. 5:26–27).

When we love our wife the way Christ loves us, we picture this good news to her, our children, and the church. But living out this testimony isn't easy—not for us, not for her. So we must continually pursue Christ: individually and together. Brother, for your wife's sake, don't neglect your spiritual health. Fight to commune with the Lord, and lead your wife to do the same.

Both you and your wife need to set aside time to read God's Word and pray that your souls would be fed. Get sufficient rest that your bodies may be refreshed. Eat a healthy diet that your bodies may be strengthened. We are whole persons, and when conflict comes, if we are not spiritually grounded, physically rested, and emotionally strong, we'll either crash under the pressure or sin in the fight.

Pray with and for One Another

Conflict reveals where our trust rests, it reveals where our hope lies, and it reveals where our help resides. To whom or to what do you turn when life gets hard? Jeanine and I have found that in times of struggle and doubt, the Psalms are a rich source of help. They teach us how to pour out our hearts to God and plead for his help amid trouble. They remind us that faithful believers can be overwhelmed with grief and that it's okay to feel hurt. They remind us that some of the most acute pain is caused by those we call friends. And they remind us how to preach the gospel to ourselves.

In some of my darkest times, Jeanine has written out specific psalms for me and pointed me to trust in the God who is always for me and never against me. She has reminded me of the specific ways she is praying for me, according to a particular psalm. In my moments of greatest weakness, she has been in my corner reminding me of the God who is still on his throne, though the ground underneath my feet is crumbling.

Protect the Church and Your Family

Unfortunately, in the midst of conflict, we'll be tempted to say hurtful, sinful things to our wife, our children, and our church. We can't control what people say to or about us, but we can control what we think and say. No matter how bad things may get, the church is still the bride of Christ, and we must protect her.

Protect the church from and for yourself. Let's be careful how we think about church members and leaders. They're Christ's sheep under our care. Let's fight by faith to think the best of them. And let's work to develop a thick skin and a soft heart. To the degree that we protect Christ's bride in our own hearts, from our own selves, we protect Christ's bride before others.

Protect the church from and for your wife. If we share with our wife every disagreement, criticism, and complaint from staff, leaders, and members, we may skew her view of individuals and even the entire church. What we share with her requires discernment that must be assessed case by case. It requires wisdom to know what she can handle and what she cannot, what will crush her and what won't. It requires integrity to maintain the promised confidentiality of church leaders and members.

Because our wife is in our corner and feels our pain, she will naturally want to fight for us and vindicate us. But it's not her fight! One of the great lessons I learned during conflict was that the Lord is my defender. That truth liberated me from having to defend myself and recruit my wife to get into the ring with me. Have open and honest conversations with your wife about what you will and will not talk about. But remind her that by not telling her everything, you are actually caring for her.

Finally, protect the church from and for your children. We know it's inappropriate to "dump" on our kids. But if they overhear us complain about leaders or church members, we will taint their view of the church. We want them to follow Christ and love the church. Therefore, during conflict protect the church for their sake. And when they witness members saying and doing sinful things, protect the church from them by pointing them to Christ and the gospel. Encourage them to pray for those who persecute you.

Practice Forgiveness and Seek Reconciliation

Sadly, during conflict, our righteous anger can quickly turn into sinful anger. If we're not careful, that sinful anger will take root and grow into bitterness. That's true for us and also for our wives. The key to battling sinful anger and uprooting bitterness is forgiveness.

All true forgiveness begins in the heart, and when we forgive those who have sinned against us, God uproots our sinful anger, kills our bitterness, frees us from taking revenge, and empowers us to love others as Christ loved us. And when we love as Christ loved us, we picture the gospel before our family, before those who sin against us, and before the church.

More Than Ever

I hate conflict, but I've learned that avoiding it only makes matters worse. Even during the most difficult times of ministry, I thank God for a godly wife who has always been in my corner. I'll close with a letter she wrote to me many years ago. It was a dark time.

> Juan,
>
> As I sit and pray for you, God's words are the most comfort. David wrote those psalms for our comfort and prayers! They are wonderful. Read Psalm 56: "Be gracious to me, O God, for man has trampled upon me. . . . In God I have put my trust. I shall not be afraid [but I still hurt deeply—JS]. What can mere man do to me?" Psalm 57: "My soul takes refuge in Thee. . . . I will sing praises. . . . My heart is steadfast." Psalm 59: "Let them be caught in their lies."
>
> I know God can do great things through this. As Mother said, "Holiness is costly." You can teach the people, lead them to handle things biblically, forgive them, and go on—whatever that may be.
>
> This is an important time for me also to fall at his feet and rely on him, which I have not done in a long time.
>
> I love you now more than ever.
>
> Jeanine

7

They've Left, and I'm Crushed!

Dave Harvey

Dear Pastor Dave,

They've left, and I'm crushed. They were faithful members—good friends I counted on. They were generous givers, committed volunteers, true servants. But now they're gone. These departures deliver blows that cut me deepest as a pastor. These wounds fester with pain.

I know leaving seemed right to them. And I know God is in control of these things. But emotionally, these experiences feel like "desertions" or "defections" or "treason." When they group up before hitting the exit, I hear incessant voices in my head reminding me of how I've failed. These voices trigger sharp pangs of grief. I know that my words are exaggerated and emotionally charged. But when a trusted friend or a long-standing member says goodbye, the news breaks over my soul like an unholy AWOL—a mission desertion. And with each parting, my heart grows more brittle.

Sure, I signed on for suffering. But I never imagined ministry would look like this. The person I poured so much time into has vanished. The relative I thought would always have my back is gone. The fellow pastor who preached about relationships abandoned our church for a better-paying ministry job. How should I interpret unexpected departures from our church? How do I handle the spontaneous separations from our congregation, the inexplicable goodbyes from people we love, or the leader who goes rogue and leaves a trail of confusion?

If I can be honest, people can be pretty unthinking when they leave. They can be entirely unaware of the knife that pierces a leader's soul. They're unaware of the fact that I lie awake at night, seeking grace just to rise and meet the next day. How do I find grace to keep going in ministry when the departures come like waves?

To cut to the heart of the matter, where is God when people leave?

Faithfully yours,

Deserted Shepherd

Dear Deserted Shepherd,

Talk to any church leader in a vulnerable moment, and you'll discover that he has a desertion story—even the big guns. "Ten years of toil," Charles Spurgeon lamented, "do not take so much life out of us as we lose in a few hours by Ahithophel, the traitor. Or Demas, the apostate."[1]

Traitors. Apostates. Defectors. Pretty bad stuff. In reality, certifiable betrayals represent only a small slice of people who leave. But each departure can leave a scar that lasts for years.

Ministry carries this paradox. People kindle our greatest joys, but they also become the cross on which we must consent to be impaled. It's an irony of Christian leadership. We are called by God to love, nurture, and care for God's people—to invest our lives in them—only to watch some reject our leadership and mash the eject

1. Charles H. Spurgeon, *Lectures to My Students* (Grand Rapids, MI: Baker, 1977), 1:175.

button. To love truly makes one vulnerable, and when a sheep is drawn away by misunderstanding or offense, the pain is acute. This is particularly true when people leaving slam the door behind them and launch a campaign that appears to revise history and lay the responsibility for their problems at the feet of their bewildered shepherd. Perhaps you've been there.

Sometimes . . . We Are to Blame

Let's be honest. Sometimes we *are* the problem. Fallen leaders fail people. Our ignorance, inexperience, sinful responses, and broken leadership are often the shove that sends people stumbling out the door. We're dull too, so we often don't connect the dots until weeks or months later. But let's face it: God's call to Christlike leadership comes with no guarantee that we will see a reciprocal Christlike followership. Our mistakes will often reverberate louder than they should. The inevitable result? People we love will leave. And with them goes a small slice of our heart.

The question is, How does a leader stave off cynicism? How do we carry on without feeling like our relationships are rigged for disappointment, like we're holding a ticking time bomb? Some pastors don't. They just bail out. Others keep going, but they become "professionals," building an impenetrable firewall between God's church and their heart.

But are those the only options open for us? How does God sustain a pastor or pastor's family when people leave? And how can God furnish us with the tools needed to meet painful departures with the kind of faith that results in ministry longevity?

Remember Paul

In a dark moment of my life, while I wrestled with these questions, I picked up 2 Timothy. It's widely understood to be Paul's last will and testament. To begin, I was struck first by the number of people who abandoned Paul: "You are aware that all who are in Asia turned away from me, among whom are Phygelus and Hermogenes" (2 Tim. 1:15).

One can almost feel the distress behind his words. Paul carried the scars from these memories into the final days of his ministry.

Paul seemed to anticipate that Timothy might be skeptical: "*All* Asia has left? Surely not Phygelus and Hermogenes?" "*Yes, even Phygelus and Hermogenes.* Even *the oldest comrades* walked away." Note this well: departures are never abstract. They have names and faces. Pastors limp when people leave. That's the way it was for Paul, and it's the way it is for us. And Paul was just getting started:

> But avoid irreverent babble, for it will lead people into more and more ungodliness, and their talk will spread like gangrene. *Among them are Hymenaeus and Philetus, who have swerved from the truth,* saying that the resurrection has already happened. *They are upsetting the faith of some.* (2 Tim. 2:16–18)

Hymanaeus and Philetus—two leaders clearly known to Timothy as well. We don't really know what memories were triggered by the mention of their names. Was it late nights sharing burdens around the fire? Was it ministry experiences where God moved in powerful ways? We don't know what nostalgic levers those names pulled. But we do know that they departed from the truth; they were destroying the faith of some.

Do you have a Hymanaeus or Philetus in your ministry, revising doctrine to fit his or her desires, rallying saints to a vision grander and more glorious than your old and outmoded one? It's not a new story. But in this dark night of my soul, that Paul shared this story sparked something in me. As I read and reread these chapters, an ember of hope kindled in my heart. Even Paul, arguably the most gifted and faithful leader in Christian history, endured the same rejection as I did. But there was more:

> Do your best to come to me soon. For Demas, in love with this present world, has deserted me and gone to Thessalonica. Crescens has gone to Galatia, Titus to Dalmatia. Luke alone is with me. . . . Alexander the coppersmith did me great harm; the Lord

> will repay him according to his deeds. . . . At my first defense no one came to stand by me, but all deserted me. (2 Tim. 4:9–11, 14, 16)

Tap the brakes for a moment—Paul had a few more names to add to the list of deserters. It's even more personal than we initially imagined. Paul loved people. Losing Demas to the world or becoming the target of Alexander's abuse wasn't just another day at the office for Paul. These were vexing relational burdens, a cross he had to consent to carry.

Paul still hadn't hit bottom. "No one came to stand by me, but all deserted me" (2 Tim. 4:16). Have you ever been in a situation where your credibility is under attack and your explanations prove useless? A season when insult follows injury and no one steps forward to support you? That's where Paul's story went. In one of the darkest and most desperate moments, when Paul's faith and ministry were under indescribable assault, he stood alone. Next time you wonder whether anyone can truly understand the crushing sense of loss you feel from the departure of a member, the betrayal of a leader, or an unexpected abandonment, remember Paul.

Illusion of Resolution

None of us signed up to have our ministry stories end like Paul's. It's all so unresolved, so humiliating, so, I don't know, open ended. No one taught me this in seminary or elder training. None of my teachers told me, "You'll experience radical conversions, restored marriages, the power of the gospel moving in the lives of people . . . and oh, by the way, there will be inexplicable departures that will rip your heart out!" I just figured if we were all gospel centered, sincere, and reasonably faithful, our churches would grow, people would dig us, and our ministry stories would end well. Ministry pain is supposed to resolve, isn't it?

When I looked honestly at Paul's last epistle, it blew these expectations apart. His final chapter is awash in complexity. Unresolved relational grief. Departures. Desertions. Apostasies. Lots of people bailing out. No tidy bows. No closure.

Here's the hard truth every pastor must steel himself to face: The cross on which you must consent to be impaled is *people*. Serving them will inspire indescribable joy, but that service will also rend your heart and escort you into unimaginably dark nights of fear, grief, anxiety, and sorrow. Times when you long for resolution that you simply will not experience this side of eternity. When a leader's affliction remains open ended, where does he look to find meaning?

How Does a Leader Consent to Be Impaled?

The departures catalogued in 2 Timothy are no coincidence. They serve as a point of continuity—heartbreaking and soul-shaping continuity—between Paul's pain and your pastorate. Because under the lash of these defections, Paul points us back to the one whose earthly ministry included the anguish of abandonment and the agony of distressing departures. Paul lifts the head of the disappointed pastor and turns it toward Jesus's invitation to take up your cross and follow him (Matt. 16:24). The summons from the Savior is to lay down your defenses, pry open your heart, and consent to be impaled. Follow Jesus in his descent to the dead, not because we glory in anguish but because we know that this suffering and death are only the prelude to the beauty and miracle of resurrection life.

So when departures come and our world feels like "all Asia has deserted," how do we give God our consent and follow the Savior in his sufferings?

Affirm That God Has Packed These Departures with Purpose

God is not sitting idly by in heaven, passively observing these separations. He's not up there fretting over the kingdom setback inflicted on his designs by this desertion from your flock. No, God is sovereign. He is behind the steering wheel on all partings.

If that doesn't comfort you, I understand. In leading a church, I noticed that the closer I was to the person leaving, the less this doctrine consoled me and the harder it was to trust God's providence—at least initially. The more that individual service, influence, or gifting drove the church's vision, the more difficult it was to trust the Lord. *Why?* became an elusive, unanswered question that enticed me with distraction and disappointment.

Paul got it, though he seemed to share our ignorance. There's no indication that Paul knew why "all Asia left him" or why at his first defense "no one came to stand by him, but all deserted him." People fled Paul like he was radioactive, and yet there were no enlightened lessons to be found as he surveyed the wreckage of these desertions, no "aha" moment to surprise him (or us!) with satisfying clarity.

I recently met with a pastor who was going through a really difficult time. Good folks were leaving, his church was being shaken, and he was shuddering under that low-grade anxiety that accompanies constant criticism. As a way to humbly learn and care for those who were leaving, he conducted exit interviews, inviting folks to share their reasons. The exercise, he reported, was both illuminating and perplexing—illuminating because he heard some valid concerns, perplexing because the issues, at least to him, didn't seem significant enough to warrant a mass exodus.

In time, clarity may come. A day may arrive, in fact, when you are able to see a direct connection between your leadership and your members' farewell. But for now, allow God to meet you in the mystery. See it as an opportunity to know Christ in the fellowship of his sufferings and to commune with him (Phil. 3:10). Trust him with your loss. I know you don't see it, but this departure is brimming with purpose.

Paul saw God's purpose. It was the ground on which he finally set his feet in 2 Timothy. After his long list of departures, he writes,

> But the Lord stood by me and strengthened me, so that through me the message might be fully proclaimed and all the Gentiles might hear it. So I was rescued from the lion's mouth. The Lord

> will rescue me from every evil deed and bring me safely into his heavenly kingdom. (2 Tim. 4:17–18).

Paul was deserted, but he was not alone. He was forsaken by men, only to be rescued by God. The Lord was there, standing by him.

Jesus went to the grave, but he didn't remain there. He rose, and he stands today alongside lonely leaders. Maybe that seems like hollow hope to you right now. "Great, the Lord is with me. My divine silent partner—dragging me along in my worst times in some spooky 'footsteps in the sand' fashion." Hold on, look closely at what Paul says. The Lord strengthened him so that he could carry on the mission with power. The Lord didn't just arrive—he came in like a divine Delta Force to rescue Paul with overwhelming firepower. The evil deeds of errant leaders would not prevail. The painful grief from lost friendship would not dominate his mind when he stood to give his defense, because Jesus was standing by and would one day take Paul safely home.

The abandoned moment became a rescue story, an experience of power for mission, a promise of grace to sustain, a commitment to deliver Paul safely. That's a whole lot of wonder packed into one experience of desolation.

Remember That Leading Faithfully Is More Important Than Being Right

The local church gets the best of who we are as pastors and church leaders. We signed up knowing that. Our sense of calling carried an expectation of sacrifices. In Paul's own words, we would "spend and be spent" (2 Cor. 12:15) for our people. This was never just a job. It was a sacred assignment.

But when folks leave casually, cruelly, or sinfully, leaders face a unique danger in the wake of their exit. We can lose perspective, take it personally, or even equate leaving our church with leaving God's will. From there it's only a hop, skip, and jump to defending ourselves and demonizing those who depart.

Sometimes they make it easy. People can sin grievously in their conduct toward the church or in the way they decide to leave. The flesh catches fire and burns with slander, quarreling, and divisiveness. There's no hurt like "church hurt," and there's no ugly like "church ugly." Folks can say goodbye with fiery words that torch the bridge, hoping the blaze reaches your reputation. "Alexander the coppersmith," Paul lamented, "did me great harm" (2 Tim. 4:14). Alexanders come to us all. When they punch, we want to counter. When they rant, we want to retort. When they accuse, we want vindication.

Paul could relate, but he chose another way: "The Lord will repay him (Alexander) according to his deeds" (2 Tim. 4:14). When it came to leadership, Paul played the long game. He didn't hold God hostage to vindicating him or assume God had to prove his divine goodness by clearing Paul's name. Instead, Paul followed the path of Jesus: "When he was reviled, he did not revile in return; when he suffered, he did not threaten, but continued entrusting himself to him who judges justly" (1 Pet. 2:23). Despite what he had walked through, Paul trusted his vindication to the Lord and let Alexander be a cross on which he consented to be impaled.

In thirty-three years of pastoring, I've had some Alexanders. Each time they disappear, my heart response is unswervingly predictable. Being right can be way too important to me. I want to be seen as the righteous party. I want to fight for the correct narrative—to be vindicated from harmful slander. Justice, after all, should be served. This self-righteous attitude can lead me to say really unhelpful things. There have been times I've forgotten that once someone decides to leave, the opportunity to convince them of my "take" has evaporated. I've burned a few bridges unnecessarily, bridges that if left intact might have helped the person cross more easily back into our church.

I hope you'll receive this piece of council from a grizzled veteran pastor. Don't confuse leaving your church with leaving the gospel. And never let the fervor that rightfully belongs to the gospel be transferred over to your church or to your version of the narrative. I can fairly assume that my own rightness was the very thing that once separated me from God: "All [my] righteous deeds are like a polluted garment" (Isa. 64:6). When I'm clinging to self-vindication, I need to flee to the righteousness that comes from another (Rom. 3:26).

One important qualifying remark here. Paul wasn't personally polluted by Alexander, but his sense of responsibility for Timothy and his readers obliged him to convey a warning: "Beware of him yourself, for he strongly opposed our message" (2 Tim. 4:15). He gave a clear caution with a simple explanation. For Paul, leading faithfully meant, when necessary, tagging the wolf.

To follow Jesus is to accept the burden of suffering at the hands of people. Paul prepared Timothy for this inevitability when he wrote, "Indeed, all who desire to live a godly life in Christ Jesus will be persecuted, while evil people and impostors will go on from bad to worse, deceiving and being deceived" (2 Tim. 3:12–13). When under personal attack, the gospel outlines a distinct path of response: "Love your enemies, do good to those who hate you, bless those who curse you, pray for those who abuse you" (Luke 6:27–28).

We're able to do this because we are "sons of the Most High, [who] is kind to the ungrateful and the evil" (Luke 6:35). But there are times when the evil behavior of a defector like Alexander transcends the borders of personal assault and begins to obscure the gospel or divide the church. In those times, denying or accommodating evil behavior only perpetuates the problem and endangers the flock. Faithful leadership requires immediate first aid. Leaders must follow Paul's example of clear caution and simple explanation to stop the bleeding and keep infection from spreading to others.

Know That Closure Is Overrated

No one cares to admit it, but in a broken world, closure is hard to achieve. Paul certainly didn't die with it. It's hard to read 2 Timothy and believe that all these relationships wrapped up neatly before his death. God did not tie a bow on the pain, the complexity, the ministry absurdities. Do you think faith guarantees delivery on closure? Well, Paul had faith. The heroes of faith in Hebrews 11 had faith. But Hebrews 11:13 still says, "These all died in faith, not having received the things promised." These faithful leaders died with unfulfilled promises, unsatisfied dreams, and unanswered questions. They didn't die with resolution. They stood in faith without it.

Pastor, do you have complicated, unresolved, open-ended relationships in ministry? King David did:

> For it is not an enemy who taunts me—
> then I could bear it;
> it is not an adversary who deals insolently with me—
> then I could hide from him.
> But it is you, a man, my equal,
> my companion, my familiar friend.
> We used to take sweet counsel together;
> within God's house we walked in the throng. (Ps. 55:12–14)

Paul did too. Ministry is messy. Sometimes your best efforts at peace don't deliver the resolution you desire.

Real faith doesn't need to trace everything out. Faith doesn't demand the psychological satisfaction of resolution in our stories. Faith trusts in what God has revealed. And the most important thing God has revealed provides the answer for the closure we so desperately desire.

The gospel represents God's closure on the most important open-ended matters of the universe. In Christ, we have resolution on the crisis of sin and hope in the great and coming day when all will be made right. When a lack of resolution pollutes the present, we go back to what Christ accomplished on Golgotha and look forward to the promises of a new heaven and new earth. So when I'm trying to settle the turbulence that swells within as people leave, I must flee to the risen Savior. In Christ, I am reminded that because of his remarkable love, there is an end to my journey of pastoral desertion, a place awaiting me where "I shall know fully, even as I have been fully known" (1 Cor. 13:12).

Yes, closure will come. But not today.

Hope for Pastoral Pain

Pastor, that pain you feel, that stinging pang in your stomach that wells up each time you remember the friend who left—convert that aching moment into a reminder that there is a day coming when you will be reconciled. There's a day coming when closure will happen.

Paul expresses this confidence in his final words. He closes 2 Timothy with a doxology. From his prison cell, amid a mass desertion, Paul worships: "The Lord will rescue me from every evil deed and bring me safely into his heavenly kingdom. To him be the glory forever and ever. Amen" (2 Tim. 4:18). Despite what he's walked through, Paul is able to entrust his unresolved pain to the Lord in confidence that there's something better ahead.

I don't understand why one of your team members bailed on you. I don't know why that close friend left your church. I don't know why that leader you poured so much time into deserted you. I don't know why the faithful members who pledged their undying support and loyalty no longer attend your church.

But I can say this: when you feel that stab of betrayal slice deep into your heart and yet still trust the goodness of God; when you stand up to preach knowing some people are gone for good; when you wipe tears from your eyes before the next meeting but still carry on the living, the loving, and the leading—the pain that you are bearing then, that very cross on which you consent to be impaled, will have a mysterious, supernatural benefit for you and for all those to whom you are called to serve. It's why Paul was able to confess with full assurance, "But the Lord stood by me and strengthened me so that through me the message might be fully proclaimed" (2 Tim. 4:17).

God's presence and power are yours, even when—and especially when—people have left and you're crushed. It's all you're promised for the day of desertion. But it is enough.

8

Does Staying in a Small Rural Church Make Me a Failure?

Mark McCullough

Dear Pastor Mark,

I hope this finds you well, dear brother. Today marks the twentieth anniversary of my arrival here as pastor of this church. I'll never forget how eager I was to serve as a pastor and how happy my young (and smaller, in those days) family was to transition from seminary to a small rural church like the one I continue to serve today.

I pray that I have served this congregation well these past two decades, that I have preached God's Word faithfully, that I have loved them fully, but I must admit something: I'm surprised that I'm still here. On the day the congregation elected me, there were eighty people on the membership rolls. Today, there's ninety-two. That's not much difference. Sure, there have been several people who joined us over the years, and there have been a few conversions too, but there have also been some who haven't remained with us.

The small town our church serves is a macrocosm of our church. Population in the entire county was 12,000 when I first began, and today it sits at 9,800—not much happening here, and our young people always seem to leave for the city and the opportunities it offers for careers and, as much as I hate to say it, more prominent churches and preachers.

Honestly—and I hope this doesn't sound prideful—I always thought I would serve a larger congregation in a more highly populated—and more significant—place. It seems nowadays, too, that a pastor has to build his platform through social media, but I haven't really done that, because nobody is going to read the musings of a pastor serving in such an obscure place. Same with books—I have ideas, but who would ever read me when you have so many other good options by pastors who preach before hundreds and thousands each week?

Now that I've reached middle age, I sometimes wonder what might have been. Have you ever felt this way? Should I think about making a change at this juncture, maybe look for a new position in a larger place? Or is there genuine merit in doing the same thing week in and week out for the same people for a lifetime? As you can probably tell, I'm beyond discouraged and am being tempted by anxious thoughts about what I've accomplished for the Lord.

Your wisdom would be much appreciated in this moment.

Blessings,

Obscure Pastor

Dear Obscure Pastor,

Your question, as I understand it, is, How can we be filled with joyful contentment in pastoral ministry even when our setting is one of anonymity and obscurity?

That's a great question—and important, because it addresses a tension most of us face. On the one hand, I would suppose we all, at least occasionally, wonder what it would be like to be widely known in ministry circles. That's understandable. Fame is not a bad thing in itself. I have a number of spiritual heroes. (Several are contributors to this volume!) And their "fame" is the vehicle God used to bring the blessing of their influence to me in my remote setting. I praise God for their fame! And just as their being widely known has been the occasion of great blessing to me, I can only imagine what a thrill it would have been to know that God had used me to bless so many.

But the fact is, few of us called to ministry will ever be famous. And many—if not most—of us will labor our whole lives in settings where no one outside our churches will ever know our names.

Is Contentment Even Possible?

You're wondering if it's possible to be content in such an environment. If our contentment depended on our being widely known, then contentment would certainly be an impossibility. The good news is that true contentment does not depend on the breadth of our ministry. I know that for a fact. God sovereignly and graciously placed me in my current pastorate nearly three decades ago. We have witnessed the problems plaguing much of rural America—the shuttering of manufacturing plants, negative population shifts, and school closings. And I have to admit my inability to protect our church from being affected by many of these changes.

I'm certain that few outside my isolated church field will ever know my name. Yet God has been faithful through it all to sustain within me an ever-deepening sense of contentment.

So, yes, I would say that it *is* possible to be deeply and joyfully content even when no one outside your church will ever know your name. The question is how.

It seems that at the heart of your question is the idea of "being known." I think that shows us the way forward. It has been my experience that we can overflow with joyful contentment in all circumstances if we simply abandon the futile effort to seek contentment through "being known by others" and focus instead on three superior joys.

Three Superior Joys

The Joy of Knowing and Being Known by God

The first—and most important—key to contentment is to focus on the irrepressible joy found in knowing God and being known by him.

In knowing him, we find a joy that no amount of fame could ever afford—and no degree of obscurity can ever take away. Through the years, I've been encouraged by passages like Jeremiah 17:5–8. Its words wonderfully address the question before us:

> Thus says the LORD:
>
> "Cursed is the man who trusts in man
> and makes flesh his strength,
> whose heart turns away from the LORD.
> He is like a shrub in the desert,
> and shall not see any good come.
> He shall dwell in the parched places of the wilderness,
> in an uninhabited salt land.
> "Blessed is the man who trusts in the LORD,
> whose trust is the LORD.
> He is like a tree planted by water,
> that sends out its roots by the stream,
> and does not fear when heat comes,
> for its leaves remain green,
> and is not anxious in the year of drought,
> for it does not cease to bear fruit."

Jeremiah's warning in 17:5–6 speaks directly to your issue. When we look to the approval of man and seek that approval by our own machinations, aren't we guilty of "trust[ing] in man" and having hearts that are turning "away from the LORD"? Certainly. And what does he tell us will result from this misguided aim? Not contentment but spiritual barrenness. We will become "like [shrubs] in the desert," and we "shall not see any" of the good we desire come to pass. If we pursue contentment by means of men's applause, then we will certainly (emotionally and spiritually) live in the desert, in the parched places of the wilderness, in an uninhabited salt land. We'll be destined to experience the exact opposite of what we seek.

But what a magnificent promise the prophet holds out for us in the next verses! If we turn from trust in man to place our trust in the Lord, if our focus is not on being known by man but on knowing God and being known by him, look at the results. There's a spiritual vitality and fruitfulness certain to afford us contentment—regardless of our circumstances.

I strongly encourage you to memorize and meditate frequently on this and similar passages (e.g., Psalm 1). They will send "rivers" of contentment-producing power flooding into your heart. I have found that to the degree I immerse myself daily in the pursuit of joy in God—and by grace am enabled to know and enjoy him—I discover that desires for the praise of man are driven from my consciousness. Let me encourage you to place the highest possible priority on knowing and enjoying God. Use all God's means of grace to the fullest extent possible in your fight for joy in God.

There is real freedom in this grace. When we spend ample time in communion with him through the Word and prayer, he fills us to overflowing with his joy. That sets us free to focus all our efforts on serving others. And don't forget the words of Jesus: "For even the Son of Man came not to be served but to serve, and to give his life as a ransom for many" (Mark 10:45). Wanting to be noticed by others and wanting others to make much of us and meet our needs are a prescription for pastoral frustration.

Unfortunately, I've often heard pastor friends voice a desire to move on to another church because their current church does not sufficiently appreciate them or "do enough for them." But if your joy is based on how much others are taking notice of you and meeting your needs, then you're going to be frustrated more often than not! Lack of contentment can absolutely kill our effectiveness in ministry.

We must also bask in the joy of being known by God. God has often used his Word to assure me that *he* knows me, that *he* takes notice of me and my ministry. I'm thinking, for example, of Colossians 3:22–24. Paul is speaking there to "bondservants" about what should and should not motivate them in their work:

> Bondservants, obey in everything those who are your earthly masters, not by way of eye-service, as people-pleasers, but with sincerity of heart, fearing the Lord. Whatever you do, work heartily, as for the Lord and not for men, knowing that from the Lord you will receive the inheritance as your reward. You are serving the Lord Christ.

We who are privileged to be in ministry are also "bondservants" of the Lord. We should do our "work heartily, as for the Lord and not for men." We know that the Lord is watching our work and that nothing we do in service to him goes unnoticed by him.

How can I be full of contentment even when no one outside my church will ever know my name? One big reason is that my Lord knows me. I can easily handle the fact that "no one outside my church knows my name" as long as I know that *he* does.

The Joy of Making God Known

Another key for contentment in quiet, out-of-the-way ministry settings is the joy of making God known in the place where he has planted us.

There is great joy to be found in abandoning the endeavor to *be* known in favor of the far more fulfilling aim to make *God* known. This second key flows out of the first. As we search the Scriptures daily, seeking to know God better and praying that he will "make known [to us] the riches of his glory" (Rom. 9:23), God graciously shows us more and more of his beauty. This beauty fills our hearts so that we find great contentment-producing joy in sharing with others what God shows us about himself and his great salvation.

Often our sense of contentment is threatened when God, in his good and wise providence, calls us to endure a "lean season" despite our best efforts to proclaim Christ and invite sinners to him. And one factor that can fuel discontentment during these seasons is our tendency to compare our situations and capabilities with those of other pastors. I recall a conversation some years ago with a gifted and faithful pastor from another part of our state. He told me that in the fast-growing area where he ministered, his church averaged twenty-five visitors each Sunday, mostly believers looking for a church home. If even a fraction of those visitors became members, he said, they were certain to have a "fast-growing church" on their hands. Obviously, not every situation fits that pattern. We must not envy pastor brothers who minister in such situations. Certainly, they face challenges we know nothing of.

Just as we should not torpedo our own contentment by comparing our geographic and demographic situations with those of other servants, we should also avoid comparing our giftedness and temperamental tendencies. I've known and highly admired faithful men who were gifted to accomplish great things in their churches in a remarkably short span of time. I've often marveled at the gifts of such men—while being painfully aware that I'm not one of them. Yet I have sensed that, by God's grace, he has gifted me (and called me) to devote myself to a ministry demanding patience and perseverance over the long haul.

We have "gifts that differ according to the grace given to us" (Rom. 12:6). Much contentment can be found—especially during difficult seasons—by simply allowing God to give us clear insight into the gift mix he has granted us and then trusting him to give us grace to use those gifts as best we can in the situations where he has seen fit to station us.

The Joy of Knowing Others

The final key God has used to sustain contentment in my obscure ministry setting is the joy found in knowing others.

Great contentment results when we lay aside the ambition to *be* known and instead pursue the far more rewarding joy of knowing others—really knowing, loving, and caring for others, especially the people we're privileged to shepherd. These joys are multiplied when God calls us to the high privilege of devoting our labors to a particular people over a lifetime. These joys to me are increasingly inexpressible as the years file by.

There is a depth of love and joy between pastor and people that only a "long marriage" can produce. How wonderful when, in God's plan, he gives us those years! God has differing plans for different pastors. But it's best not to prematurely pass over the significance of God's sovereignty in placing us where we currently serve.

We must be ready to depart immediately for other fields of service should God lead us to do so, but we must also be so content in him and so full of love for our flocks that we're delighted to serve them for a lifetime should that prove to be God's will for us.

I'm incredibly grateful that God has allowed me to stay where I am all these years. Incomparable delights result when God gives us such a love for a people and such joy in knowing *them* that we grow oblivious to the fact that no one outside our church will ever know *our* names.

Let me give you a couple of examples. Jesslyn—that's a name I delight to know, the name given to a baby girl born about a quarter of a century ago. How privileged I felt to be with her family at the hospital the morning she arrived, to see and share their joy. Another name I rejoice to know is Gaston—that's the name Jesslyn gave to *her* firstborn son twenty-something years later. How gracious of God to allow me to be with Jesslyn (and her family) both on the day of her birth and on the day she first gave birth. Those are the kinds of gifts God gives us when he graces us with long pastorates.

Gerald—that's another name I love to know, the name of a man attending our church when we arrived nearly three decades ago. He was what you might call a "good man." He was a man of towering physical strength, an outdoorsman, a hard worker, a good provider. He evidenced no marks of regeneration. He had a stern, intimidating countenance. Honestly, I feared him. His life apart from Christ took a toll on his marriage, but he had a godly, praying wife who never gave up on him—and never gave up on God, praying for her husband without ceasing. God gave me the privilege of sharing the gospel with him and witnessing his radical conversion. His marriage was saved, and he blossomed into a faithful servant of Christ and his church. He never lost his strength but added to it a beautiful quality of gentleness.

Two and a half years ago, he was diagnosed with an aggressive, incurable form of cancer. He proceeded to walk that dark journey with victorious faith, and like Abraham, "he grew strong in his faith as he gave glory to God" (Rom. 4:20). What a privilege it was for me to walk that journey with him, one that recently led to "the river's edge." There on the banks of that river, we fed together on passages like Psalm 27:1: "The Lord is my light and salvation; whom shall I fear?" And I thrilled to hear his words to us all, assuring us that through his faith in Christ alone, he had "no guilt in life, no fear in death" and was "ready to go home." It was as if he were calling to me from the midst of "the river" to let me know that he could "feel the bottom, and it was good." How grateful I was to preach the gospel to all who gathered to honor my friend Gerald's memory and to see his widow radiant with joy through her faith in the Savior I've been privileged to commend to her all these years.

Here's my point: I'm convinced that the opportunity to know people like Jesslyn and Gerald—and to walk the long journey with them and their families—has brought me far more joy and contentment than any amount of notoriety ever could.

In nearly thirty years of belonging to my beloved church family, I have found my heart increasingly knitted to theirs. We have shared so many experiences. They have grieved with my family in our losses, and we have felt theirs. The losses my people absorb are my losses. Their gains, my gains. We are truly one in heart. One people. One family—in Christ.

May all these joys be yours in abundance. And may "the joy of the Lord [be] your strength" (Neh. 8:10) as you serve him!

9

I'm Feeling Tired, Worn Out, and in Need of a Break

John Starke

Dear Pastor John,

You've been in ministry for decades, so surely you've faced my present dilemma. To risk a vast understatement, I'm tired. No, I'm physically, mentally, and spiritually worn out. I often feel as if I might collapse. Is this normal in ministry? If God has called me, shouldn't I be refreshed each week by studying and teaching God's Word?

Recently, I shared my sentiments with another pastor, and his reply left me feeling no small level of guilt. He told me, "The devil doesn't take a vacation, so I don't either. There should be no break from pastoral ministry." What do you make of that statement? Is it a sin for a pastor to feel this way and to want a holiday? I told him I'm not sure we should let the devil determine our schedule. He didn't buy it, saying, "I've never taken a vacation." He's been in ministry for decades too. Is his answer sensible? Should I feel such guilt over my profound sense of burnout?

My doctor fears that I'm on the verge of some sort of breakdown. I even had an MRI this week, which revealed that I'm showing stroke-like symptoms due to anxiety and stress. What should I do? Do I need to take a break? Should it be short or long? Please advise, as I'm beginning to feel more than a little desperate.

Faithfully yours,

Worn-Out Shepherd

Dear Worn-Out Shepherd,

You're not alone. I don't have any particular stats on the rate of burnout and exhaustion among pastors, but from experience and anecdotal observations, it's high. My guess is that pastors forsake rest because they see a day off primarily as a day designed for *recovery from* or *precaution against* exhaustion. This creates a good bit of personal justification to rarely rest, because ambition or fear can provide enough adrenaline rushing through you that you'll never "feel" exhausted. You will, then, always just keep working.

But what if the Sabbath was originally intended for something more than just recovery from and precaution against exhaustion? Many of us have created enough theological justifications for why we are not obligated to keep the Sabbath laws. Our sinful hearts have somehow learned to never take a Sabbath, and in doing so, we grind away joylessly in our toil and wonder why we never feel gratitude about our work. I want to suggest that we begin to think differently about Sabbath rest.

In the mystery novel *Still Life* by Louise Penny, Inspector Gamache, an old veteran detective, takes a calculated risk in a murder case. It backfires, getting him suspended. His badge and gun are taken away. Suddenly, without his badge and gun, he feels vulnerable and afraid. The voices of his insecure youth rise from the depths: the badge meant he was *somebody*. It had given him significance and made him feel important. Without it, he is nobody; he is nothing. He remembers an old analogy a mentor once told him, that

> living our lives was like living in a long house. We entered as babies at one end, and we exited when our time came. And in between we moved through this one, great, long room. Everyone we ever met, and every thought and action lived in that room with us. Until we made peace with the less agreeable parts of our past they'd continue to heckle us from way down the long house. And sometimes the really loud, obnoxious ones told us what to do, directing our actions even years later.[1]

Gamache wasn't sure he agreed with that analogy until the moment he had to place his badge on his supervisor's desk. Then that insecure young man lived again and whispered, "You're nothing without it. What will people think?" Realizing how inappropriate the reaction was didn't banish the fearful young man from Gamache's long house. The question for Gamache was, Would that voice be in charge?

That insecure voice directs us as pastors more than we'd like to admit. It follows us every time we go to a meeting, every time we enter the pulpit—"You are nothing without their approval; they must not see your weakness." And not only that voice but also the voices of every critic, every angry email. Will those voices be in charge? Our busyness can stuff those voices down, maybe muffle them a bit. But busyness doesn't heal a person, and those voices will likely direct us in more unconscious ways than we realize.

The Sabbath, however, does something terrifying at first. It brings stillness and quiet so that all the ghosts and goblins of our insecurities and anxieties come to the surface. And maybe you think to yourself in those moments, *This is why I don't do this sort*

1. Louise Penny, *Still Life* (New York: St. Martin's Paperbacks, 2005), 205.

of thing! But it's only then that these things can be cast on Christ and that he can begin to heal them. His voice becomes a more directing, comforting voice. In discussing the Sabbath, Judith Shulevitz writes, "Not only [does] drudgery give way to festivity, family gatherings and occasionally worship, but the machinery of self-censorship shuts down, too, *stilling the eternal inner murmur of self-reproach.*"[2] Stilling the eternal inner murmur of self-reproach. You need that.

Rethinking the Sabbath

Have you ever watched people (maybe yourself) try to do too much? They never stop, they never rest, and you say something like, "You're trying to be like God!" It's true that they aren't living within their human limitations. But it isn't God they're trying to be like. In fact, God himself tells us to model our work and our rest after him. Eugene Peterson explains that if we are made in his image, we will want to watch his creation week closely.[3]

Notice in Genesis 1 that God didn't pile all his work into one day. He could have, but instead he took it one day at a time. First, he made the sun and moon, night and day. That was a good first day. He stood back, like an artist from his work, and said, "It's good." The second day he separated the water from the land. He again made note of the goodness. The third day was plant life. It was good. The fourth day he made the stars and shaped the light to create seasons. The fifth day was flying birds and swimming creatures. The sixth was animals and his final crowning achievement, man. It was all good, he said. Very good.

God wasn't in a hurry, but he never procrastinated. Have you ever noticed that Jesus acted this way during his earthly ministry? He healed lines of people, but then at some point in the day, he stopped, rested, prayed, and ate. He left many needs un-

2. Judith Shulevitz, "Bring Back the Sabbath," *New York Times*, August 21, 2003, https://www.nytimes.com/2003/03/02/magazine/bring-back-the-sabbath.html.

3. Eugene H. Peterson, *Christ Plays in Ten Thousand Places: A Conversation in Spiritual Theology* (Grand Rapids, MI: Eerdmans, 2008), 65–82.

addressed. Jesus was never in a hurry, and Jesus never procrastinated. When we are in a hurry and never rest, it isn't God we are acting like.

"Watch me," God says. He worked six days and rested. You think he was tired when he rested? No. If God rested even though he wasn't tired, and if he asks his image bearers to rest like he rested, do you think maybe there's a deeper reason for rest than mere exhaustion?

Look at the pattern in Genesis 1. God created man on the sixth day, rested on the seventh, and some time after that, commissioned us to work. The first act of man was not work but a participation in rest.

Pastor, you are made in the image of God. When you work, watch God. Be holy as your Father in heaven is holy. He worked six days and rested. Yes, we are free from the law, but we are not free from the command to be like him.

Sabbath and Busyness as Catechesis

How you engage with rest will function as a kind of catechism of the heart. Whether you give in to a culture of busyness or engage in rhythms of Sabbath rest, both will form you into a certain kind of person. We don't like to think of it that way. We'd like to think that our books and our sermons are doing all the formation, but unfortunately, that isn't true. How we spend our time both exposes what we truly love and forms us in what we love.

We live in an age of efficiency, and pastors have swallowed this cultural pill with a big glass of water. We judge our use of time by what gets produced. Were we productive? Did we get something done? Did I check something off my to-do list? Productivity is king, and efficiency is our mistress. Pastors sanctify it by calling it "redeeming the time." The problem is that if this is how we will judge our time, we will never justify using it for spiritual practices like prayer. When the Psalms talk about prayer, they use the language of listening, watching, waiting, or longing. Those are not efficient uses of time. Resting is even worse.

Let me ask this: Do you feel lazy when you take a day off? Indulgent? Do you see pictures online of other pastors taking days regularly for themselves and wonder, consciously or unconsciously, if they ever get anything done? I want to suggest that if you tend toward these questions and thoughts, you have been formed by our culture of efficiency.

We lie to ourselves and say that since we are doing spiritual work, we won't need rest. It's too important. We admire pastors who pass out in exhaustion over their sermon notes, who burn out, who work themselves into the ground, who have no other interests but theology and books. Who has taught us this way? What dark catechism are we learning from that glorifies workaholism?

The creation account shows us that God designed us to be fruitful and productive. "I want you to be like me," he says, and he creates us in his image. "But one of the ways in which I am going to ensure that you do not make work the most important thing—to keep it from becoming 'god' in your life—is that I want you to rest." Our culture teaches us that you ought never to put down your work. The Sabbath is a catechism teaching us that God is the only one whom we ought never to put down.

Along with embracing a culture of chronic efficiency, pastors have also come to believe that they hold the church together. If the pastor begins to take normal, regular rhythms of rest, things will begin to fall apart or slow down, momentum will stall, and your email inbox will grow out of control. Somewhere we have learned to think that if we just keep working, the church is safe, and the gates of hell will not overcome. We would never say these things aloud or even whisper them in the dark, but our relentless late nights give us away.

We must learn that trusting and resting go hand in hand. Taking a Sabbath rest is our expression of faith. "He must say farewell," Abraham Heschel says, "to manual work and learn to understand that the world has already been created and will survive without the help of man."[4] Let's reword that for pastors: "A pastor must take a day of rest, in which he says farewell to pastoral duties and learns that the church has already been built and will survive without his help." To be in a hurry, always busy, never resting is a compulsive grasping for things we were never meant to possess or control.

Sabbath Healing

Our reasons for not resting are often more superficial than we think. Yes, you may be busy, but there are more likely deeper reasons. For many of us, the reason we resist stillness and rest is because that's when the ghosts and goblins of our fears, anxieties, and insecurities come to the surface. Busyness is our best defense against them. It has done a good job so far at keeping them at bay, but we must confess together that busyness never heals us. At some point, we'll need to be still, rest, and let Jesus heal the hurt inside. That won't happen fast, and maybe rest will look more like restlessness at first (that's my story). But Sabbath healings come. Marva Dawn encourages us, "When clergy realize that their congregations can get along without them just fine for one day a week, then they are freed to be obedient to God's design for well being."[5]

Dan Allender describes participating in Sabbath rest as remembering the garden and rehearsing new creation.[6] For those of us who need healing but are fearful or anxious about what comes out of us when we rest, consider your Sabbath as garden remembrances and new creation rehearsals.

Remember

Whenever God calls us to remember the Sabbath and keep it holy, he often reminds us of the original creational Sabbath he celebrated:

---

4. Abraham Joshua Heschel, *The Sabbath: Its Meaning for the Modern Man* (New York: Farrar, Straus, and Giroux, 2005), 264.
5. Marva Dawn, *The Sense of the Call: A Sabbath Way of Life for Those Who Serve God, the Church, and the World* (Grand Rapids, MI: Eerdmans, 2006), 53.
6. Dan Allender, *Sabbath*, Ancient Practices Series (Nashville: Thomas Nelson, 2010), 55.

> Remember the Sabbath day, to keep it holy. Six days you shall labor, and do all your work, but the seventh day is a Sabbath to the Lord your God. On it you shall not do any work, you, or your son, or your daughter, your male servant, or your female servant, or your livestock, or the sojourner who is within your gates. For in six days the Lord made heaven and earth, the sea, and all that is in them, and rested on the seventh day. Therefore the Lord blessed the Sabbath day and made it holy. (Ex. 20:8–11)

God is calling us to remember. Remember the time I rested? You ought to remember those original days, those original times of innocence and delight. In the garden there was no grief, no sin, no worries, no anxieties, no division, only life and love. There was perfect communion between God and his people. Here's the point: The Sabbath is a time to remember when humans didn't have to prove themselves worthy. Each day was a gift to receive.

Today, we pastors feel this inner necessity to overextend our competencies and overpromise. Why? We agree to cover and accomplish things we have no business taking on. On the Sabbath we remember when humans didn't need to overextend their competencies and overpromise. They were just themselves and were loved. Can you imagine?

I've picked up a discipline that's gone a long way in helping me. And I think it could help you too. In the creation narrative, God seems to be making notes throughout the week about what's good, what to celebrate, what worked. He created the sun—*it is good*; he made the stars and moon—*it is good*; he made the land, the oceans, the animals, the birds, mankind—*it's all good*. It's like he had a work journal, so that by the end of the week, he stood back, with everything he had made, looking at his notes, and said with a deep breath, "It's all *very* good."

I began doing likewise. Each morning in my prayers, I would take a few minutes and write down what was good from my work the day before. What worked? What was worth celebrating? What was fruitful? What was good? What are all the reasons to give thanks?

Where was the Lord present? How was my work participating in the kingdom of God?

At the end of my work week, my family brings in our Sabbath rest through a dinner—a good dinner, something we all love, with special drinks, around the table. Maybe we'll share it with a few good friends. Each will share what he or she is thankful for in the past week. We describe what was worth celebrating and where we saw God's grace among us. And I have my list from the week ready.

Something like this is important because pastors can grumble. Can you believe it? We can feel used, ignored, unworthy, unfruitful, like a failure. Sometimes criticism crushes us. But each Thursday evening I sit down with my family, and I have these notes where I have seen God at work, where my labors were fruitful, where the joy of the Lord was my strength and it was good. It helps me put down my work and rest.

Rehearse New Creation

Keeping the Sabbath holy is rehearsing the truth that some day God will make all things right. Justice will be restored, relationships will be reconciled, and our bodies will be healed. What we'll be like, we don't exactly know. But we do know that "when he appears we shall be like him" (1 John 3:2). The world will be new, and we will be like Christ. The Sabbath is a day to rehearse. This means we treat those in our community as if they will be in Christ, beautified in glory. We set aside tensions for the day. We overlook offenses. We assume the best of one another and give each other the benefit of the doubt. It doesn't mean tensions and pain simply go away. It could be that you'll need to pick up those tensions the next day and work toward reconciliation. But having what's eternally true in Christ (peace, reconciliation, and joy) inform for a day what is momentarily and experientially untrue now has a way of healing and restoring. Something of the kingdom breaks in and heals us.

It's a mystery, but it's God's way of doing things.

Abraham Heschel tells a parable:

> A prince was once sent into captivity and compelled to live anonymously among rude and illiterate people. Years passed, and he languished with longing for his royal father, for his native land. One day a secret communication reached him in which his father promised to bring him back to the palace, *urging him not to unlearn his princely manner*. Great was the joy of the prince, and he was eager to celebrate the day. But no one is able to celebrate alone. So he invited the people to the local tavern and ordered ample food and drinks for all of them. It was a sumptuous feast, and they were all full of rejoicing; the people because of the drinks and the prince in anticipation of his return to the palace.[7]

Do you see? The prince was rehearsing his princely manner and the joy of the palace so that he would not forget what he would be like again. That's the Sabbath. Rehearsing what's coming, rehearsing what's eternally already true in Christ. It's rehearsing our princely manner so we don't forget, because, oh, how we forget.

Sabbath is a remembrance of the garden, where we feasted with God in the cool of the day, and a rehearsal of new creation, where we will feast with him in the new world. The Sabbath is a day for joy and delight. A day to buy too much food and share it. A day to eat, drink, and be merry because we're going to live forever!

Pastor, you need it. You have a spiritual and theological justification to have the best day of the year once a week. Don't wait until you're exhausted to take a Sabbath. That's not primarily what the Sabbath is for. The Sabbath is a day to delight in something deeper than your work.

7. Heschel, *Sabbath,* 346.

10

My Church Has Outgrown My Gifts

Scott Patty

Dear Pastor Scott,

Oh, how our great and mighty God has blessed our congregation in recent days. Ten years ago, we planted this work with barely enough people to hold a Lord's Day worship service. I remember those first few years when we were thrilled to number fifty on a Sunday, and then in year three we reached one hundred and felt like we had arrived. At that point, we were confident the church would remain for many years, planted on a firm foundation. These past few years, the Lord has certainly honored his Word and has grown our church and expanded this ministry far beyond anything I could ever have imagined.

And our neighborhood is growing as well. In those early years, this district was what one might call a small town or even consider an out-of-the-way place, but that is no longer the case. Today, it's part of our city's growth corridor. By God's grace, our church and the surrounding community seem to be expanding along parallel tracks.

However, and this is the real purpose for my letter, another notion has become abundantly clear to me these past few months: I'm not certain if I have grown as a leader to the same degree, at least not enough to competently manage the current demands of our church. This body looks entirely different from when I first cast a vision for it. Now we have more than fifty small groups, and we add numerous Sunday school classes every few months. Throw in nearly forty students from the local seminary who need mentoring and new ministries in areas of outreach to the poor and broken, new-believer discipleship, and the ever-growing need for counseling, and I'm feeling utterly defeated.

Honestly, I'm just not sure I have the range of gifts needed to lead this congregation any further. Moving forward, I'm wondering if our people might be better served by a lead pastor whose vision and abilities are dynamic and match the church as it exists today—not as it was a decade ago. Back then, I was confident that God had fitted me for this calling. Today? I'm not so sure. Our church is now complex and unwieldy. Should I resign and seek a venue of ministry that better fits my gifts?

All this has left me perplexed and ridden with anxiety. Your wisdom is desperately needed on this matter. I eagerly await your answer.

Faithfully your son in Christ,

Deep in Doubting Castle

Dear Deep in Doubting Castle,

My moment of doubt came at 2 a.m. I, too, questioned my calling to continue to serve my congregation. I sat at my desk depressed and anxious as my family slept. I asked the Lord if maybe there was someone else who could lead the congregation better than I could. I wondered if the time had come for me to step aside for the good of the church. I didn't want to resign. I loved my church. I was the founding pastor and had served with gifted and sacrificial elders and church members for eight years. We were friends. I had no plans to move to another location or to a different type of ministry. I simply wondered if I was holding back the church.

At this particular time, the issue was our congregation's need for a more permanent location and building for weekly worship and ministry. We had wandered around our city for years without a place to call home. I saw the wear and tear on our congregation of physically setting up facilities each week. I began to notice a restlessness among us because we didn't know where our ministry home was located. The problem, in my mind, was that I hadn't successfully led our congregation to secure land or a building. I wasn't sure I could. While the church was having good and normal growing pains, I was having a leadership crisis.

There have been other seasons as the pastor here when I questioned my ability to lead. The issues causing concern were related to growth in some seasons and little growth in others, difficulty securing staff, navigating differences among church members over certain cultural and political issues, personal insecurity about my preaching and pastoral care, and not having enough energy to accomplish all I believed was expected of me. In each case, your question was my question: Do I have the gifts needed to lead and shepherd this growing congregation?

I encourage you to see your growing congregation as an opportunity for your growth in at least three areas: a heart of humility and faith, wisdom for perspective on your situation, and leadership ability.

Growth in the Heart

An important place to look in times of trial, doubt, and tension is within: What is the state of your heart?

It's good to get straight in our minds that the church belongs to Christ. He, as the head, leads it. He causes the growth and keeps his church in faith. Knowing that Christ leads and keeps his church will not relieve us of our pastoral responsibility and the need to develop necessary skills. It will, however, lead us to greater humility and faith. We'll be less inclined to exaggerate our importance and more inclined to believe that he can work through our less-than-stellar leadership abilities.

When humility lives in our hearts, we come to see that we are never fully equipped to do the real work of ministry, which is in the souls of people. This is always God's work. As we are effective in our own personal soul work, God can better use us to bring his Word to bear on the consciences of people by the power of his Spirit. In humility we depend on the Lord for all aspects of pastoral work. Humility is a necessary quality for receiving what we need from God to do his work.

Humility will also free us to let others help us in the work. The problem is not our inability to do everything. Not allowing others to help, guide, or even lead us is the problem. Developing the ability to lead a team is important, but before we will increase in ability, we must grow in humility.

We also need to grow in faith. Where there is faith in the heart, the Word of God is trusted. We equip ourselves with the Word, and we lead our churches with the Word. Preaching and teaching the Word are understood to be at the heart of pastoral leadership.

We cannot forget that God intends to build our faith, not just the faith of those in our congregation. The leadership crises we face are one of his ways of doing so. One day in the midst of a particularly difficult leadership challenge, I inwardly wished it would simply go away. I asked God to remove it. The next thought that entered my mind was, *God will not orchestrate circumstances in my life that do not require faith.* I took that as the wisdom one-liner that I needed at that moment. I have returned to it many times.

Asking God to work humility and faith in our hearts may clear up misperceptions about our ministry, our situation, and ourselves. This clarifying process may show us that we actually can lead the congregation we currently serve—not as a super CEO but as a person of vision and energy, qualities that flow from a receptive and expectant heart. We may find that the way forward is through personal revival rather than by tweaking our leadership style and strategy.

Before concluding that your church has outgrown your ability to lead it, spend time with God and open yourself to humility and faith-building work. Ask him to help you lead with heart.

Growth in Wisdom

Closely related to growth in humility and faith is growth in wisdom. Wisdom gives us a new perspective, leading to a different approach to the situation at hand.

It's wise to realize that we don't really need some of the things we think we must have to lead a congregation. This is a matter of expectation.

We often assume that to be effective in ministry, we must have a certain personality type or work with a specific leadership style. But is that really true? Does God make all pastors alike in personality and leadership style? Jesus didn't choose apostles who were all alike. Church history doesn't show one ideal pastoral type that was most effective. We need wisdom to see that God calls and equips different kinds of pastors with various leadership styles because there are many types of people in the world and in the church. People respond differently to different pastors. Particular situations call for unique pastors. Knowing this reality will help us get our expectations under control and may lead us to see that we really don't have a problem after all. We can lead our congregation as we are because we may be exactly what our congregation needs.

It's wise to remember that there are places that we don't need to take our congregations. A pastor may be laboring under the expectation that he must lead his church to be like another church, to build another building, to develop a large staff, or to have a certain worship style. These expectations may be self-imposed or put on him by others. Whatever the source, such expectations must be examined. If found to be unnecessary, they can be dropped. The pastor and the congregation are now free to see clearly what they are to do in keeping with the mission of Christ's church.

It's unwise to compare ourselves and our congregations to others. Comparison, whether favorable or unfavorable, is not a good way to develop vision. Comparison leads to pride or to increased expectation on ourselves, and then to greater discouragement. Rejoice with others in their success, pray for others when they fail, and keep your eyes on the work before you.

Wisdom helps us see that not every pastor and congregation will look the same, because not every city or ministry setting is identical. Many pastors in urban settings are discouraged because their congregations are not situated in facilities like the ones their suburban friends enjoy. This may affect the congregation's numerical growth and size. It's easy for these pastors to assume that this is a leadership issue when it's simply a land- and parking-availability issue. Wisdom will help these pastors see that they are uniquely gifted to lead specific ministries that will advance the kingdom in their particular setting.

Growing in wisdom can also help us see that we cannot lead alone. We must lead with a team. God has given many wise and capable people to his church. Elders are needed. Deacons and staff members can take a share of the load. Church members are the ones who really do the ministry (Eph. 4:12). The wise pastor prioritizes the development of these teams and servants in the church.

The wise pastor also remembers that the main goal is to lead people to Jesus. We often overemphasize organizational leadership skills and underemphasize the pastoral skills of preaching, having conversations, and praying with people. Keeping the main emphasis on leading people to Jesus doesn't mean we accept poorly led organizations as the norm, but it does remind us that we don't have to be able to run a massive corporation to be an effective pastor. We do, however, need to know Jesus and be able to lead others to him.

Before leaving a congregation for issues related to leadership, the wise pastor will pray for wisdom, get the perspective of wise people, and sort out what expectations need to be released. Ask the Lord to give you greater wisdom for great effectiveness right where you are.

Growth in Leadership Ability

With humility and faith in the heart and the clear perspective that wisdom gives us, we can take an honest look at our leadership ability. If we come up short, we can humbly acknowledge it, commit ourselves to grow, and make a plan. I encourage you to focus your leadership growth in three areas: personal management, team development, and the necessary skills to be the voice of vision for your church.

Leadership ability begins with personal leadership and management. A wise mentor once gave me a course on life management and encouraged me to invest the time needed to master a few patterns and practices that would be helpful to me. The few weeks I invested in that program have paid tremendous dividends in ministry effectiveness.

There are many books and online training programs available to help you grow in personal management. The good ones focus on mission and purpose before offering time-management solutions. Good leaders and managers let their mission and purpose determine their roles and responsibilities, which then will guide what activities actually make it onto their calendar. They understand that the point is never just good time management but better life management. We are not to simply fill up time with activity; we are to determine what activities are necessary to fulfill our purpose and then schedule them in the best way possible.

To grow with your congregation, you will need to make sure you are managing your life according to mission, purpose, roles, and responsibilities. Then you will need to work these things into your schedule for sustainable time management. Find a good resource to help you grow.

Commit to grow in your ability to develop and lead teams. Church planters and solo pastors learn a necessary skill at the beginning of their ministry: how to work alone. But as the congregation grows, they need to learn how to work with people. When we started the church I currently serve, I did many of the jobs required for weekly ministry. Checking the church post office box, printing bulletins, preparing to preach, calling volunteers, and setting up chairs were tasks that I moved in and out of with ease. But with growth in the church, I soon realized that I needed a new skill set. I needed to develop teams of people to do the work. I spent time reading and learning about the work of elders, deacons, volunteer leaders, and paid staff members. I developed the ability to transition from working alone to working with people. Now I work with people who know far more than I do about organizational management, money, communications, and technology. I work with volunteers who know more about pastoral ministry than I do. What a gift from the Lord!

Take the long view in this work of team building. You'll need time to identify the right people to lead and serve with you. It'll take time to give them vision and training. You'll need to replace them often because of changes and transitions. A commitment to building the right team will make up for your lack of ability to lead in many areas of ministry. It's not your ability as a solo servant that matters most but the collective abilities of the congregation. Find good training for building teams in your church.

Focus your leadership work on being the voice of vision for your congregation. Work hard at preaching and teaching the Word. Lift up the glory of God and the beauty of the gospel. Communicate the mission of the church. Set the pace in discipling others. Make the big decisions that shape the culture of the church to be biblical and healthy. Be a Christian among your people. Show them what humility, love, and service are about. These things provide vision for people. People need vision.

You will want to grow in leadership abilities because doing so will give you the opportunity to be the voice of vision for more people. Your leadership abilities are to be in the service of Christ and the vision he has for his people. Before you assume that you don't have the ability to lead your congregation, commit to grow as a leader.

Leave or Stay?

A growing congregation requires a growing pastor. Heart growth in humility and faith, wisdom growth for perspective, and growth in leadership abilities are key areas for every pastor to pursue.

Still, it's possible that a pastor simply cannot be effective in a certain context because either he doesn't possess the necessary abilities to do so or he possesses a different set of abilities than his setting needs. So he may need to move on. This doesn't mean he has failed. Our sovereign God can use this challenging situation to further refine a pastor and lead him to pursue a more suitable place to serve where he will be happy in the work.

A church in my city called a new pastor after the previous man had served a long and fruitful tenure. The new pastor soon came to see that his gifts didn't match the needs of the church. His heart was in a good place. He sought wisdom for his situation. But the skills needed for the job were different from the ones he possessed or could reasonably develop. After a few years and many honest prayer meetings with the Lord, he left that church and went to another where he flourished.

My 2 a.m. prayer meeting led to a different result. I stayed, and I remain pastor after twenty-five years. But the main point is this: the Lord is sovereign over his church. When we are seeking his glory, not ours, and when we want to serve others, not ourselves, we can trust that he will lead us in the decision to leave or stay. And we can rest assured that he will give us what we need either way.

11

How Am I Going to Make It Financially?

Brandon Shields

Dear Pastor Brandon,

I hope this finds you prospering in the Lord. I am writing to you about prosperity—a lack of it in my case. The ministry trouble I'm experiencing now relates to money. No wonder Scripture says so much about this topic. My church plant is doing fine financially, but my family is struggling. We have four children, have incurred some medical bills of late, have a mortgage, and have incurred lots of other expenses related to providing the basics for a family. But my pastor's salary is just not cutting it. At the end of the month, the amount needed to provide our needs always seems to outstretch my income by a good bit.

How do I work through this? I know God has called me to be a breadwinner for my family and also to pastor a local church, yet one doesn't seem congruent with the other. What should I do? Should I ask for a raise? Find a ministry position that pays more? Get a second job? Talking about money makes me feel incredibly guilty, because I realize ministry is not about money. Still, my family has to eat!

My education and experience are completely ministry related, so getting a second job would be a tough task. I'm not even sure it would really help, and it would only tire me out further and risk lowering my energy level (and time available) for preaching and shepherding my congregation. Also, how can I guard my heart so that I don't become obsessive, extremely stingy, or worse? How can I deal with this guilt? It's so hard for a pastor to talk about money. I'm afraid my congregation will merely view me as greedy. Will ministry ever meet my family's needs? Am I just thinking wrongly about all this?

Your advice is desperately needed, as my family seems to sit on the edge of financial ruin.

Faithfully your son in the faith,

Going Broke

Dear Going Broke,

For the first decade of pastoral ministry, I enjoyed the luxury of never having to worry about money. Working in several affluent megachurches afforded my family a premium salary, generous insurance and retirement benefits, and huge margins for savings. Seven years ago, however, we experienced a financial crash.

When our decision to plant a church in urban Indianapolis forced a massive pay cut and a savings account depletion, my security was threatened for the first time as an adult. The financial habits that I had considered virtuous for much of my life—hard work, aggressive saving, minimal spending, and calculated generosity—worked for me in the prosperity of my previous context. But in the face of this unexpected financial strain, I became obsessive, controlling, and manipulative with my family's finances. Something had to change, but I had no idea where to start.

Recently, I was leading a conversation on ministry finances with some young pastors in my city and asked them, "Is your current compensation sustainable for your family's next season of life?" Unsurprisingly, all of them said no. "If you could have a candid conversation with the people responsible for setting your compensation, how much would you need to make to support your family at a reasonable level?" Their answers reflected what I've consistently observed over the last several years—if these pastors didn't receive a substantial increase in their salaries, they would need to pick up a side hustle, look for another church, or leave ministry altogether.

Universal Problem

People commonly struggle with financial fragility and insecurity. Many are quietly suffering through the pains of paying the mortgage, figuring out how to educate their kids, and finding margin for the latest emergency. If pastors buy into the false narrative that nobody understands us, we risk feeding feelings of resentment. As leadership consultant Edwin Friedman points out in his work *Generation to Generation*,

> Clergy families neither exceed nor lack their quota of the human family's problems. . . . They are not unique in the way they are affected by the forces of society: inflation, scarcity, the women's movement, inner city, or suburbia. . . . The emphasis on how clergy families are different sociologically allows members of those families to avoid seeing their own role in their own victimization. The blame can more easily be placed on situational factors, and the failure to cope is more easily disguised by rationalizations.[1]

Unfortunately, our cultural milieu makes it nearly impossible to talk about real financial struggles, because we are saddled with so much shame. While it may be true that we live in the "age of authenticity"

---

1. Edwin H. Friedman, *Generation to Generation: Family Process in Church and Synagogue* (New York: Guilford, 1985), 278, 281.

when it comes to issues like food, sex, power, and politics, there's still nothing that will more quickly turn a dinner party awkward than a question like "How much money did you make last year?"

Honest and specific conversations about one's financial situation are some of the few remaining taboos in the West. In his explosive article "The Secret Shame of Middle-Class Americans," author Neil Gabler struck a cultural nerve with his raw vulnerability:

> You wouldn't know any of that to look at me. I like to think I appear reasonably prosperous. Nor would you know it to look at my résumé. I have had a passably good career as a writer—five books, hundreds of articles published, a number of awards and fellowships, and a small (very small) but respectable reputation. You wouldn't even know it to look at my tax return. I am nowhere near rich, but I have typically made a solid middle— or even, at times, upper-middle-class income, which is about all a writer can expect, even a writer who also teaches and lectures and writes television scripts, as I do. And you certainly wouldn't know it to talk to me, because the last thing I would ever do— until now—is admit to financial insecurity or, as I think of it, "financial impotence," because it has many of the characteristics of sexual impotence, not least of which is the desperate need to mask it and pretend everything is going swimmingly. . . . To struggle financially is a source of shame, a daily humiliation— even a form of social suicide. Silence is the only protection.[2]

Problems Unique to Pastors

The recognition of universal struggles, however, doesn't negate the existence of some unique financial constraints on ministry families. Every vocation has its own set of "occupational hazards." Let me highlight several that operate unconsciously in the social architecture of a local congregation.

---

2. Neil Gabler, "The Secret Shame of Middle-Class Americans," *New Yorker*, May 2016, https://www.theatlantic.com/magazine/archive/2016/05/my-secret-shame/476415/.

First, local church ministry can place a constraint on wealth-building opportunities as typically defined in America. In most modern work environments, employee compensation is directly tied to measurable performance indicators like sales, profit, technical competency, billable hours, networking, overtime, and industry experience. Success in these areas leads to financial incentives like promotions, bonuses, stock options, equity, and even lucrative consulting gigs that help build long-term wealth "airbags."

Ministry, on the other hand, operates with a different set of rules. Churches are nonprofit organizations whose budgets are limited by external factors. Generally, pastoral compensation is determined by a constellation of subjective measures unrelated to performance: tradition, cost of living, level of seminary education, preaching aptitude, or even perceived reputation. "Ministry success" is ill-defined, and the lack of financial incentives creates a low ceiling for long-term wealth-building opportunities like savings, investments, retirement, or college funds.

Second, local church ministry can place a financial constraint on pastors' wives. Despite the fact that more than 60 percent of families with children younger than eighteen in the United States are now dual income, some congregations still hold an unspoken expectation that a pastor's wife doesn't work outside the home and doesn't receive any compensation for work she does for the church. Although in some contexts pastors' wives may find it desirable or necessary to work exclusively at home, the archetypical traditional family structure is a social pressure few outside the church must manage. This assumption puts pressure on single-income families. Consider how it makes women and children financially vulnerable to tragic pastoral failures such as addiction, depression, suicide, and adultery.

Conspiracy of Silence

As if these problems are not discouraging enough, there's a deeper, more dystopian shadow at work—nobody is allowed to talk about any of it! Denominations, missions agencies, and financial teams are not bringing the conversation to their pastors, nor are many of my pastor friends initiating the conversation with their leadership teams. How do we live and lead those trusting us if we are unwilling or unable to discuss the truth about money?

When we attempt to ignore money or deny its power in our lives, we ironically end up empowering its dark side. Unable to articulate the stories and feelings that shape our relationship with money, we become complicit in the conspiracy of silence plaguing a number of churches and pastors' families.

I first encountered this weird silence in a conversation with a ministry friend who served at another megachurch. While describing his church's hiring process, he said, "We don't share compensation information before hiring someone. We don't want money to be a factor in a person's decision to take this job. We want them to trust God to provide for their needs."

As a person who didn't grow up in the church, who ran my own lawn business as a teenager, and who majored in business during college, I found this conversation bizarre and naive. It exposed some of the unspoken assumptions that pastors face with money in the church. Is it really a lack of faith to inquire about the details of compensation before accepting a ministry role? Why would trusting God preclude the exercise of one's God-given mental faculties to discern whether a particular opportunity is a good stewardship decision for one's family? How much should money factor into a decision to accept a ministry calling? Who determines what constitutes a reasonable standard of living for pastoral ministry?

While many pastors choose to suffer silently, the reality is that these struggles conspire to create regular feelings of anxiety, isolation, and powerlessness.

Money Tells a Story

Financial anxiety is an ancient problem. In Matthew 6:19–34, Jesus identifies our compulsively anxious relationship to money as one of the barriers that hinders our ability to experience the good life of the kingdom: "You cannot serve God and money. Therefore, I tell you, do not be anxious about your life" (Matt. 6:24–25). Jesus invites us to see that money is not some commodity we make to secure goods and services—it's a primal power that can also make us insecure.

Money functions like a narrator or storyteller—it excavates the hidden motivations, values, myths, and longings that unconsciously drive our patterns of feeling, thinking, and behaving. In other words, how we relate to money reveals more than our financial principles; it uncovers our true ambitions. Money shines a bright light into our inner world, illuminating a complex ecosystem of spiritual and emotional narratives: fear, guilt, shame, joy, godly desire, selfish ambition, security, comfort, scarcity, abundance, and a legion of others. This phase of discovery, young pastor, seems to be where you are now.

The story of money both taught and embodied in the life of Jesus is an invitation to the dual nature of human flourishing. Jesus invites us to stand in the tension of both freedom and sacrifice. By freedom, I mean the financial flexibility that offers choices aligned with our human vocation, and by sacrifice, the willingness to risk financial loss for the good of others. The tension exists in the interdependence of freedom and sacrifice—in plenty or in want—in the story of the kingdom: money "answers everything" by providing the freedom for us to enjoy what truly matters in our life as human beings (Eccles. 10:19; Phil. 4:10–19), but that freedom must always be circumscribed by solidarity and sharing with those who are most vulnerable in our sphere of influence (1 Tim. 6:17–19).

Instead of obsessing over his basic needs, Jesus enlisted a group of trusted friends who funded his ministry and freed him to love, heal, teach, and serve his disciples (Luke 8:3; John 12:1–8). Rather than accumulating privilege and status for himself, Jesus redirected his power for the benefit of the most needy through intentional acts of vulnerability and sacrifice (Luke 11; John 13). This pattern of freedom and sacrifice yielded a life of surrendered contentment that unleashed flourishing for Jesus and those whom he loved (see figure 11.1). If we are to fulfill our calling as leaders who love others with the power and presence of Jesus, then it must become our pattern as well.

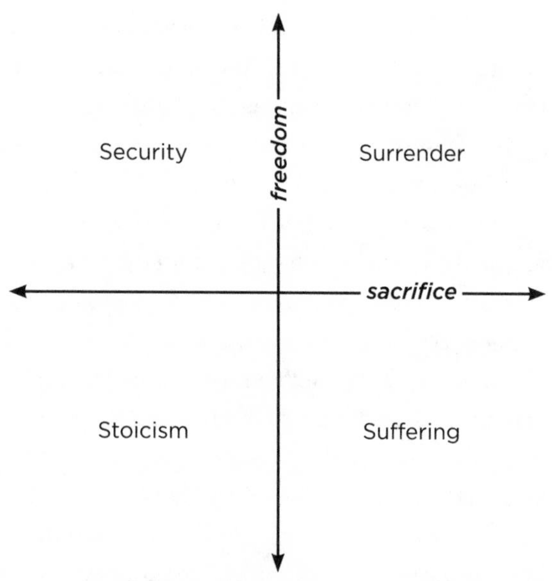

Figure 11.1 Four money stories

Three Distorted Gospels of Money

Every pastor and church has a set of organizing assumptions that provide an implicit framework for how they relate to money. The problem is that few people acknowledge the narratives that drive those assumptions. I believe the two basic narratives of money—freedom and sacrifice—provide the subtext for the financial anxiety experienced in ministry. Certain people, owing to their wiring and upbringing, are drawn toward the freedom money can provide, while others will be inclined toward self-sacrifice. However, the truth is that we need to pursue both realities if we are to flourish as human beings in our ministries.

Decoupling freedom and sacrifice leads to three distorted "gospels," or stories, that then shape faulty assumptions about money (see figure 11.1).

Gospel of Security

If we experience too much freedom without sacrifice, we can quickly become preoccupied with ourselves and isolated from the concerns of our neighbors. Ministry in this framework becomes another vehicle for pursuing our own comfort, security, and lifestyle privilege (1 Tim. 5:5–10).

Consider, for example, the assumption in some affluent megachurches that pastoral compensation should borrow purely from marketplace principles like scale and organizational value. Senior leaders are compensated like corporate executives, including lavish signing bonuses and fully loaded benefit packages. This narrow focus on compensating for security creates a lifestyle that limits risk and vulnerability for pastors and can lead to disparity, injustice, and corruption.

Gospel of Suffering

If we experience too much sacrifice without freedom, we often become overwhelmed by the needs of others while ignoring the welfare of our own families (1 Tim. 5:8). Ministry in this framework becomes martyrdom, with families feeling trapped and obligated to long hours with little pay.

I've seen this mentality play out in historically rural denominations and lean church-planting networks where the assumption is that a low ceiling should be placed on a pastor's earning potential. I have friends involuntarily living below the poverty line and making less than the minimum hourly wage while juggling multiple jobs to afford the rising costs of living in the city or supporting their children with special needs. While there is certainly nothing wrong with taking a vow of poverty, there is a tragic injustice that occurs when financial decision makers (many of whom are themselves financially benefiting from evangelical-based systems or are independently wealthy) force people into poverty without taking into consideration their unique needs and desires. This assumption robs pastors and their families of the dignity God designed them for as image-bearing humans.

Gospel of Stoicism

If we lack both freedom and sacrifice, we fall into the worst story: stoicism. Ministry in this framework feels like a cold war, where desire is stifled and everyone is passively resigned to waiting for others to make the first move. Nobody feels empowered or motivated to speak up for the financial health and well-being of the church or its leaders.

This is probably the most common narrative I witness in church planting. It's rarely intentional, but so many churches (especially younger and more idealistic communities) suppress honest money conversations. Since everyone is busy pursuing their own careers, families, and hobbies, the church lacks the urgency to set good policy and facilitate life-giving practices. The result is that pastors can be left feeling frustrated, embittered, and detached.

Leaning into the Tension

What does it look like for pastors to flourish financially? God exercised his creative power in the beginning to create a world of love that was "very good" (Gen. 1:31), and Jesus came to restore this vision of "abundant life" for everyone, including those in ministry (John 10:10). While we certainly aren't free to conflate that with the Western master narratives of individualism, capitalism, and achievement, I also think there is a subtle danger to settle for less in our ministries today than Jesus was offering. Returning to our tension, I would argue that flourishing is found in the pursuit of freedom *and* sacrifice that leads us to a place of active surrender (see figure 11.1).

This idea of resolute surrender is best captured in Anabaptist spirituality by the word *Gelassenheit*, which is a German way of combining serenity and tenacity. *Gelassenheit* transcends our weak notions of surrender as resignation or passivity, replacing them with a yielded fortitude that is both strong and submissive. I believe this is the heart of the apostle Paul's radical spirituality of money, which enabled him to speak with a refreshing boldness to the Philippian church concerning his feelings (Phil. 1:7), wounds (1:17), future hopes and expectations (1:20), anxiety (2:28), story (3:4–6), journey to contentment (4:12), and gratitude for their generosity that left him overpaid (4:18). Struggle, adversity, and surrender created the internal capacity for him to freely enjoy good times when they came and to also embrace strategic sacrifice when the situation called for it (4:11–13).

Dear pastor, rather than seeking to balance the tension of freedom and sacrifice, I want to invite you to consider leaning into the area that is most underdeveloped in your life during this season. If you've pushed too aggressively into sacrifice in a way that has left your family feeling depleted (my story), then maybe you need to lean into freedom and make some decisions that could amplify your joy. If you fall into patterns of comfort and security, then maybe the call is for you to lean into sacrifice and embrace downward mobility for the good of others. Either way, I'd strongly encourage you to invite a community of trusted friends and advisers into this process with you to help you see past some blind spots that may be keeping you from experiencing the comprehensive flourishing into which God has invited you.

Breaking the Silence

The fragility and anxiety of our cultural moment has fueled a conspiracy of financial silence that is undermining the well-being of pastors and churches. If we continue to ignore the story that money is telling us, and if we believe the lies of distorted money gospels, we will inadvertently perpetuate the legacy of shame, resentment, bitterness, and burnout illustrated by your letter.

But we have the freedom to break this taboo and choose a different legacy. If we can learn to listen to the stories money is telling, reject the distortions, and lean into the tension of freedom and sacrifice, we can flourish with the "life that is truly life" (1 Tim. 6:19 NIV)—a life full of love, integrity, abundance, and surrender to the mystery of God's good plan for our ministries.

12

I've Come to Doubt My Calling

Jeff Robinson Sr.

Dear Pastor Jeff,

I have now logged a little more than five years in pastoral ministry, yet a burning question has confronted my mind of late and has thrown a chill on my desire to persevere in ministry: Am I really called to serve in the office of pastor after all? Is this really the kind of service for which the Lord has suited me? Might it not be better for me to serve in another corner of the Lord's vineyard? I have advanced degrees in theology. Perhaps the church would be better served by my leaving and pursuing a position in Christian academia.

Why would I ask such potentially life-altering questions? Because evidence seems to be mounting that perhaps I have misunderstood God's will. Each Lord's Day, the people seem disconnected from my preaching. Some fall asleep. All look bored. There've been no converts lately. I've heard comments such as "You sound more like a lecturer than a preacher." That hurts. But is it telling? Am I called to serve as a professor instead of a pastor? Maybe. Am I called to some other form of ministry? A writer or editor? It's possible to serve the local church well in that capacity. I just don't know.

You may say, "Well, perhaps you simply need to grow as a preacher," but they just don't seem to be following me. A wise man once told me, "If you are trying to lead and nobody is following, then you are just going for a walk." Maybe that's the case for me. This just doesn't feel like success.

Have I confused a passion for the Bible, theology, and the things of God with a call to pastoral ministry? Am I merely being tempted by my flesh or the devil to flee on the next sailing vessel for Tarshish? Maybe I'm just tired of the war here and want to find peacetime there? Have you ever questioned your own calling?

Faithfully yours,

Dazed and Confused

Dear Dazed and Confused,

I can assure you that you're not the first pastor to wrestle with the question whether you're really called to pastoral ministry. It's an issue that haunted me throughout virtually the entire span of my first full-time pastorate. I spent countless hours in prayer and conversation with fellow pastors over the matter. Let me tell you a bit about those circumstances so we can ground the issue in real-world ministry, then I'll tell you what drove me to press on.

Doubts about My Calling

Two years after completing a doctoral degree in seminary, I launched out into my first full-time pastoral position. On the surface, the church that called me seemed almost utopian—it was a confessional body that espoused sound doctrine; constitutionally, it had embraced a plurality of elders; it had been led for more than two decades by a faithful expositor of God's Word; and the people seemed to delight in the preached Word, eager to grow in grace and to have my family join theirs.

Boy, did I ever misread the situation.

Beneath the surface, crouching beyond my field of vision, an ambush waited. Lurking there was serious theological and methodological disagreement among members. There were roughly three groups within the congregation warring for the church's doctrinal and practical soul—only one of them reflected my doctrine and practice. A practical threat also loomed—a financial crisis no one seemed to know about (I sincerely don't think they did), one that threatened to rob the church of its life like a hidden bandit.

Because of these and other factors too complex to mention, there was never a day of peace in that ministry. I had opponents immediately. The first week, a man accused me of politicking my way into the office of pastor at "his" church. He made it clear that his family had voted against me. There was immediate controversy with a staff member, followed by a rebuke from a fellow elder delivered through seven handwritten pages chronicling my shortcomings as a pastor. That happened after we had served together for barely three months.

Some months later, I learned that several families were secretly plotting my ouster. I tried to do everything my seminary training called for, things I had done in ministry in the past: I preached the Word book by book, verse by verse. I worked hard to develop relationships with staff and church members. My wife and I systematically invited the entire church into our home.

None of it helped. Every button I pushed seemed to be the wrong one, every card I pulled from the deck triggered opposition, even outright anger toward my family and me. I was flummoxed. My mind grew riddled with anxiety. My wife heard all the whispers and battled bitterness. At the end, depression dug its poisonous hooks deep into my heart and mind. Don't misread me—by no means did I do everything right or handle every situation well. My foolishness only fueled the fire that burned down my ministry.

Still, what on earth was God up to? As you might imagine, it wasn't long until I began to hear the still, small, devilish voice of inner doubt: Maybe I'm not really called to pastoral ministry. Maybe I went to seminary because I love big ideas and good books—ministry was never God's plan for me in the first place, and he's disciplining me for such audacious presumption. Maybe I'm really called to be a professor—or something else. I toyed with a potential secular job in my hometown.

The final—and most painful—straw came several weeks after I marked my third anniversary. After I finished preaching one Sunday morning, a fellow elder—to the shock of my family and the congregation—rose, ascended to the pulpit, and called for a vote of confidence on me as my wife and four young children looked on from the second row. His confidence in my leadership was shot—he called me "a failed leader." If I was standing on the cliff of goodbye, those words pushed me over.

The congregation remained silent and refused to vote for or against me, but at that moment I knew: this was the end; I was done here—and maybe done in ministry altogether. Seven days later, I stood in the same pulpit and read my letter of resignation, trying unsuccessfully to hold back three years of bitter tears. I'm not normally the crying type, but the dam broke, and so did I. The next morning, I told my family we were returning to my hometown, where I would restart my former career as a newspaper journalist. I was angry at the congregation—and at God. My erstwhile elder's words echoed through my brain. How could a failed leader be called to shepherd God's people?

But God's Word Called Me to Press On

I did leave that church, but I didn't quit pastoral ministry. Why? After such an unmitigated disaster, what sane person would volunteer for a second round? That's a good question. I think my answer is as simple as this: I'm called to be a pastor. And unless I am morally disqualified—when I fail to be the man Paul calls for in 1 Timothy 3 and Titus 1 in an unrepentant and egregious manner—I am called to press on in ministry in spite of significant evidence to the contrary. We serve an invisible kingdom whose progress is often equally invisible.

I came to this conclusion through close, careful, prayerful study of Scripture. As I examined some of the men whom God called in Scripture, I realized that from a strictly human vantage point, their ministries appeared to be anything but a rousing success. God often confirmed their calling through their difficulties. And it's how he reconfirmed mine. There were three Bible figures in particular whose biographies pushed me to climb back on the bucking bull of local church ministry.

Moses

Moses's body of work didn't always look like a thriving ministry. It must have seemed to him that he was neither called nor fitted to be the great prophet of Israel. In spite of his (mostly) faithful work, not much went right. The people of God didn't follow Moses. He wanted Israel to obey the law of their covenant Lord. They wanted idols. There was that ugly incident at Meribah. The people didn't exactly affirm Moses's leadership. Moses lost his cool and sinfully struck the rock twice. He was a faithful but flawed leader.

The life and ministry of Moses shows that only God gets to decide how he uses our faithfulness. If your ministry isn't prospering by worldly standards, yet you remain faithful where he's called you, that is certainly no sign that you've misunderstood the call of God.

Jeremiah

Jeremiah is often called the "weeping prophet." No wonder. Israel's response to him was tepid, to say the least. God plainly called Jeremiah, but the prophet didn't exactly receive affirmation from his congregation. Far from it; they wanted to kill him for preaching the truth:

> Come, let us make plots against Jeremiah, for the law shall not perish from the priest, nor counsel from the wise, nor the word from the prophet. Come, let us strike him with the tongue, and let us not pay attention to any of his words. (Jer. 18:18)

Jeremiah was more interested in obeying God than in seeking the applause of men. God had called him to take a wrecking ball to Israel's idolatry. He knew it but didn't always wear the role well: "Woe is me, my mother, that you bore me, a man of strife and contention to the whole land! I have not lent, nor have I borrowed, yet all of them curse me" (Jer. 15:10).

While God and your ordaining church will help confirm your call, the congregation you shepherd may not. If your greatest pleasure in ministry is the affirmation of others, then you've (perhaps unwittingly) become your own idol. Similar to marriage and parenting, ministry is an X-ray machine, exposing the idols of our hearts. We must keep our eyes riveted on hitting the ball of faithfulness, and God will take care of the affirmations. Like Jeremiah.

Paul

I think of Paul as God's crash-test dummy. Second Corinthians is virtually a handbook on the dangerous nature of the pastoral calling. For Paul, ministry was a personal holocaust; just read his litany of sufferings in 2 Corinthians 11:23–28, where his calling card was weakness. Paul understood that touting his weakness spotlighted God's power.

And look at the shape of the church to which Paul addressed 1 Corinthians, a congregation he likely planted. He certainly saw fruit growing in the hearts of the people—rotten, emaciated fruit. Theological problems galore, coupled with gluttony, drunkenness, and spiritual showboating. But a lack of fruitfulness in the people didn't amount to a lack of faithfulness in the preacher. Only God can quantify your faithfulness, and it may have to wait until glory. Paul's Corinthian letters bear this out.

Paul told his readers that there's no ministry without crucifixion. And when crucifixion comes—make no mistake, it will—it certainly doesn't mean a man on the cross is not called. To the contrary, it often confirms his call to the service of Christ via the Calvary road of affliction. It's doubtful we'll be as severely mistreated as Paul was in ministry. Yet look at his gritty words in 2 Corinthians 1:8–10. Paul feared that he might not live through his ordeal, but he did not fear that that was a sign that he was not God's called man:

> For we do not want you to be unaware, brothers, of the affliction we experienced in Asia. For we were so utterly burdened beyond our strength that we despaired of life itself. Indeed, we felt that we had received the sentence of death. But that was to make us rely not on ourselves but on God who raises the dead. He delivered us from such a deadly peril, and he will deliver us.

From a human standpoint, Moses, Jeremiah, and Paul didn't resemble a smashing success. But they understood the call.

Am I Truly Called?

Yes, my first church left me bruised and battered. Some of the people and more than one elder—out of motives they hid from me in plain sight—tried to convince me that I was no pastor. I heard numerous explanations as to my identity: I was really a seminary professor. I might be a good staff member. Maybe I should try military chaplaincy. Alluding to my preministry vocation, one even suggested that, as pastors go, I was probably a pretty good journalist. Despite all the flak, that gnawing in my gut to serve God's people flew on. That fire shut up in my bones simply wouldn't abate, and I think it was the Holy Spirit. The desire to do the work of a pastor haunted me, keeping me awake night after sleepless night. As Charles Spurgeon advised his students, that itself may be the first subjective sign of a genuine, irrevocable call to the pastorate.

Was I tempted toward bitterness? Yes, strongly. Despair? Time after time. My story is a bit unique, even strange, but I suspect that even pastors of churches that appear healthy wrestle with bitterness and despair at times. But God mercifully helped me find peace in him in the refuge of his perfect providence—not in blaming the congregation. There was sin in the congregation and sin in my heart. In Ephesians 4:32, Paul instructs us to forgive others as we've been forgiven. The Lord gave me a chance to apply that in a very vivid way. It wasn't easy, but by his grace, we remain friends with many members of our former church.

Today, I am privileged to pastor another church under more peaceful circumstances. The Lord has been merciful to me and my family. I'm grateful I didn't follow through with my plans to return to the newspaper business—newspapers aren't exactly flourishing these days anyway. When it comes to calling, there are objective aspects, as when the local church confirms your gifts and calling externally, and there are subjective aspects, as when you sense the call of God inwardly. Both are important. Here are six lessons I've learned about calling from my years in ministry. Granted, these lean toward the subjective side and are by no means absolute, but they helped me wrestle with the issue.

1. If you suffer seasons of affliction and still want to pastor, you're probably called. Affliction will either confirm your ministry or destroy it. I once met with a young man who harbored uncertainty about his calling. It didn't take me long to discover that his doubts were rooted in a minor methodological disagreement with the pastor with whom he served. This disagreement had plunged him into deep anxiety and doubt. He saw it as suffering. I saw it differently. After talking to me and a couple of other ministry friends, we all agreed that if such a relatively trifling matter made him want to quit ministry, perhaps he should reconsider his calling. Today, he is happy working outside the church, leading his family well in the Lord, and serving as a deacon in his congregation. Every vocation comes with its difficulties. If it's the difficulties that are scaring you away, then perhaps you've misunderstood the nature of gospel ministry.

2. *If the church has confirmed your gifts, and your ministry has borne at least some fruit, you're probably called.* You've seen tangible fruit from your labors—souls have been saved, believers have grown, young men have been raised up for ministry. But you've been knocked off the horse, and you're sore. Perhaps consider taking some time for healing, and then get back on the horse. After my painful foray into pastoral ministry, I took about eighteen months before entering the pastorate again. My desires for preaching God's Word and shepherding never waned, and I spent significant time in prayerful meditation pondering lessons I might learn from my previous pastorate that would benefit those I would lead in the future. This book is actually one of the fruits from that time.

3. *You might be called away from the pastorate for a season into another form of service but will return in the future.* I had a friend recently step away from pastoral ministry and go to Africa to help plant a church over the next two years. Another brother took a teaching job at a seminary and fell back from the lead elder to a lay elder position in his church. Both hope to continue as a pastor in the future—either alongside their present calling or as a return to the local church as a full-time vocation. David Platt left the Church at Brook Hills after many years as its pastor to lead the Southern Baptist Convention's International Mission Board. After a few years, he has returned as lead pastor of a church in Virginia. God may use your gifts in a wide variety of ways. I've been an editor and adjunct professor between and during pastoral gigs. God won't waste any of the gifts he's given you.

4. *Success in ministry—as defined by the world—is no certain sign of a call to ministry.* Remember, false teachers build churches that number in the thousands, while thousands of faithful pastors lead congregations with membership rolls in double digits—or less. The "superapostles" of 2 Corinthians had no small following, yet Paul rightly dismissed them as charlatans. Healthy gospel fruit is not the same thing as bloated attendance figures

and multimillion-dollar budgets, though those things don't always indicate compromise either.

5. *If you are called, the calling remains unless you're morally disqualified.* If you meet the qualifications for elders in 1 Timothy 3 and Titus 1 and seek the humility that Peter expects to typify church leaders in 1 Peter 5:1–6, then it may be the Lord's will that you press on in ministry, even though the fruit you see may not be ripening fast. Moses did. Jeremiah did. Paul did.

Spurgeon is helpful here. The Prince of Preachers told students in his pastor's school that the first sign of the "heavenly calling" is "an intense, all-absorbing desire for the work."[1] Indeed. Paul seems to concur in his counsel to Timothy, a young pastor whom he was mentoring. In 1 Timothy 4, Paul famously exhorts Timothy to keep a close eye on his life and doctrine. But first, he tells Timothy not to neglect the gift that the council of elders set him apart to deploy, telling him to "practice these things" and "immerse [himself] in them" (1 Tim. 4:15).

6. *If you are married, ask your wife.* I know, I hear your objection: this undermines complementarianism. No, this is complementarianism at its best. When things went sour in my first pastorate, my wife continued to encourage me to press on. She even exhorted me with strong words when I fell into the slough of self-pity. She reminded me that what had happened there had nothing to do with my calling and everything to do with God's goodness and mercy in sanctifying me in his laboratory of affliction—a truth she had heard me preach dozens of times. God broke me, but he made Lisa strong. She knows me best, knows my heart, knows my strengths and weaknesses, what I'm good at, what I'm not. If not for her steady encouragement, I probabably would not be a pastor today. I'm glad God gave me a godly, wise wife who's not afraid to tell me what I need to hear. I'm thankful he broke through my stubbornness and gave me ears to hear her loving (and some-

1. Charles H. Spurgeon, *Lectures to My Students* (Grand Rapids, MI: Zondervan, 1954), 26.

times firm) admonitions. Ask your wife if she thinks you're called, and then listen to her.

It's Not about You

I'm not a big fan of "life verses." Too often, they are based on a shallow reading of Scripture that fails to interpret said verse in light of its context. But shortly after I surrendered to the call to ministry in 1997, my study of Acts 20 riveted my gaze on a single verse. It's about as close to a perfect pastoral mission statement as you're ever going to read. Since it's the Word of God, it doesn't apply merely to me but is a summary of the calling of every servant of Jesus:

> But I do not account my life of any value nor as precious to myself, if only I may finish my course and the ministry that I received from the Lord Jesus, to testify to the gospel of the grace of God. (Acts 20:24)

Perhaps you're reconsidering whether all that stress and strain is really worth it. Maybe they have unmasked you as a ministerial fraud. But when you surrendered to ministry (and really when you became a Christian), you signed over the title deed of your life to Jesus. Don't give up easily, because it's not about you. Your assignment is not to build yourself a respectable middle-class life but to finish the course and the ministry given you by divine providence. Count your afflictions as joy (James 1:2), and give your life to testifying to the glorious gospel of the grace of God.

Afterword

An Interview with John MacArthur

In February 2019, John MacArthur marked the fiftieth anniversary of his service as senior pastor of Grace Community Church in Sun Valley, California. MacArthur is an author of dozens of books on theology, Christian living, expository preaching, and cultural and local church issues. He has endured much and seen even more in his years at Grace. He is indeed a man whom God has granted faithful endurance. Several months prior to his fiftieth anniversary, I had the opportunity to talk with MacArthur about persevering in ministry. That interview is captured here.

—Jeff Robinson Sr.

Jeff Robinson: You've served as pastor of Grace Community Church for nearly five decades and no doubt have walked through every danger, toil, and snare imaginable. What posed the most serious threats to your persevering in the ministry?

John MacArthur: Pastoring is really an effort to be the instrument of the Spirit of God in the sanctification of God's people to see them conformed to Christ. I often think about the fact that election is purely God's divine purpose before time, justification is a divine act in a moment, and glorification is a divine act in a moment. And in the biography of every Christian's life, sanctification is this long, drawn-out process of conformity to Christ. And the instrument of that, of course, is the Word of God and the Spirit of God through the means of the shepherding of God's people.

So I think the hardest part about pastoral ministry is the suffering Paul talks about in 2 Corinthians 11:29, where he says, "Who is weak, and I am not weak? Who is made to fall, and I am not indignant?" You know it's not about the numbers of people in your church. It's not about a successful worship service. It's not about a big event. My life sort of rises and falls in terms of gratitude and joy on the basis of what I see in the sanctifying process in God's people—the flock the Lord has given to me.

It's disappointing when you see people you've poured your life into, and you know they have had enough exposure to the truth to be maturing and faithful, and yet they are unfaithful or sinful or, even worse, sometimes mutinous in the life of the church, doing what they can to fight against leadership and cause division. On the positive side, the greatest joy is to see someone come to Christ and then flourish and grow into Christlikeness. The opposite of that is the most difficult thing to deal with, and sometimes you wind up questioning whether you're the right person—maybe they need someone else speaking into their life. Particularly if you've been in the same place for a long, long time, you're wondering if they've heard you so much, you sort of don't have any influence left.

I think that for an enduring, long-term ministry, you live long with the wonderful, even multigenerational, blessings. I've stood by the bed of a dying, beautiful, sweet lady, from a precious family, whom I've known for decades. She and her husband are now both in heaven. Her children are in the church, her grandchildren are in the church, and now her great-grandchildren are coming into the church and being ministered to and nurtured as children. This is an incredible blessing—to see a church have the kind of continuity where it brings joy to somebody like that who's looking down three more generations. On the other hand, the downside is, you've got people exposed to the same kind of ministry, that same kind of fellowship, and they seem never to get on the path of sanctification and demonstrate much progress. That can be discouraging.

Robinson: You've preached book by book, verse by verse for decades. How have you sought to keep growing in your ability to preach and in your passion for the task itself? How can we keep our preaching from growing stale?

MacArthur: I started preaching when I was young; my first sermon would probably be sixty years ago. I've found that what energizes me at preaching is the bottomless treasure of Scripture. It doesn't matter how many times I go back to it. It doesn't matter how many times I reexamine a passage. It's an inexhaustible diamond mine. I just keep finding diamonds all over the place, and they have multiple facets. I would say at this point, at my age, I am more enthusiastic, more passionate about the things I preach than maybe I've ever been. And I've always been enthusiastic about it.

But I still love the process of discovery. That keeps me fresh. I'm still trying to understand every nuance of every passage and every doctrine. I just would say after all these years in the Word of God, week after week, day after day, sixty years of this kind of preaching, the Word is more precious to me now than it's ever been before, and preaching it is a greater privilege than it's ever been. It's now possible for me not only to prepare but also to draw from a well of the past that informs me even as I'm preaching. So there's a kind of richness in my own experience. I think if I was on the road, and I had twenty-five sermons and I was going all over the place preaching the same twenty-five, I'd wither and die. Or if

I changed churches every seven or eight or nine years and I recycled the same sermons, I don't think that would give me anywhere near the joy and the blessing of having to preach for fifty years to the same people every Sunday morning and Sunday night and know that I can't just repeat what I've said because they've already recorded it.

This has put me on course to continually search to understand the Scripture and the truth it yields better and better. It isn't the exercise of preaching that I love. I'm happy to do that. It's the privilege of proclaiming what I'm discovering. So it's the discovering process that's really underneath everything and is the reason I've stayed at Grace, other than that I haven't had a lot of offers. The other reason I've stayed at Grace is that I was afraid I would forfeit this freshness that being at the same place forces me into, and it has been the most incredible blessing in my life.

Robinson: How have you approached your devotional life through the years, and how can a pastor remain fervent day in and day out, year in and year out in his use of God's ordained means of grace?

MacArthur: I've never really been able to see the difference between studying the Scripture to truly understand what it means so I can communicate it to somebody else and a devotional approach. So if I'm reading it, I stop and say, "What does this mean?" That's just the way I'm hardwired. The study energizes me. But on the side of study, just reading Scripture is important. Through all these years, I've tried to do that in many different ways.

But I do two other things at a devotional level. I've loved reading biographies of people God has uniquely blessed, because I always wanted to compare myself with others whom I saw as far beyond me in their walk with the Lord and in their usefulness to him. So I love the sort of humbling effect of standing in the shadow of someone God has used in a mighty way, whether it's David Brainerd, William Tyndale, or whoever.

And the other thing is to read rich doctrinal material, whether it's an article, a systematic theology section, or a book on a given doctrine. That's what my heart reaches out for in a devotional sense. Many years ago when I was in seminary, I got a copy of Stephen Charnock's *The Existence and Attributes of God.* And I didn't know that anybody could have that many thoughts about God at the time. I was young. . . . I just read Sinclair Ferguson's book *The Whole Christ,* and it enriched my grasp on sanctification and antinomianism.

Robinson: Over a long haul, how do we keep Christ and the gospel at the center of our ministries and keep other things from crowding them out?

MacArthur: On the road to Emmaus, Jesus said, "Look, I'm the theme of the Old Testament," and he went into the Law, the Prophets, and the Holy Writings and spoke to them of all the things concerning himself. It's anticipation of Christ in the Old Testament, it's incarnation in the Gospels, it's proclamation in the book of Acts, it's explanation in the Epistles, it's glorification or exaltation in the book of Revelation. If you're a sequential expositor, you never get far away from Christ. You may be looking directly into his face in Matthew, Mark, Luke, and John. You're then hearing his gospel being proclaimed throughout the book of Acts. If you preach through the New Testament, by the time you finish the book of Acts, you haven't taken a breath without Jesus Christ being at the center of it. Then you get into the Epistles, and immediately they're explaining who he is and why he came and what he accomplished.

The reason I do sequential exposition of books is because I'm afraid not to, because every word of God is true. If you do that, Christ is the unending theme of absolutely everything. You know this is where your focus has to be: as you gaze at his glory, you're changed into his image from one level of glory to the next by the Lord who is the Spirit (2 Cor. 3:18). I remember finishing the

Gospel of John for a second time. I had preached through Matthew, Luke, then Mark. . . . I did the Gospel of John for a second time because many who had joined the church hadn't been there when I first did it. I finished John and said, "What would you want to do after this?" And they said, "Now we know the fullness of Christ in the New Testament. We think it would be wonderful to go into the Old Testament and find him there." It's sort of like finding Waldo—you can't find him if you don't know what he looks like. But when you know what he looks like . . . you find Christ everywhere.

When the people have a glimpse of Christ in his full glory, they desire that, and I've never found any subject, any person even remotely close to him who's better for the sake of my own sanctification and the sanctification of our people.

Robinson: Much has been written about pastoral burnout, and at least some of it seems linked to wrong expectations and disappointment. How can young ministers overcome that challenge?

MacArthur: The idea that you're going to leave the ministry out of disappointment is a failure to understand that it was never about you; it was a service to which you were called. If you were in the military and your job was to stand and guard the food while everybody else went to battle, and you were a good soldier, you'd be there doing your duty, doing what you'd be commanded to do. You'd be honored to be in the triumph in the big picture. I think we let too many guys get away with leaving the ministry because of some personal dissatisfaction. I think that can be fueled by a failure to be in the Word of God, a failure to be a faithful expositor. So I tell young guys, "Look, the first two or three years of your ministry, do exposition, work hard, go deep into the text, pour yourself into that, and you'll start good habits. Those habits will take over, and it won't depend on self-discipline in the future—it'll just be a habit. You just do it because you do it. And once you establish those kinds of consistent habits, that will sustain you through those hard times."

If you don't have those kinds of habits established in the early years, it's harder to survive disappointment. Again, it goes back to trust in the Word of God, trust in the purposes of God, the call of God where he's placed you. Be faithful to the Lord, be grateful for the service to him. Let him take care of the results. I've often said, you take care of the depth of your ministry, let God take care of the breadth of it. Someone came up to the renowned evangelist D. L. Moody, I think, a famous preacher or maybe someone else, and said, "My congregation is too small," and he said, "Maybe it's as large as you'd like to give an account for at the day of judgment." So I used to say, "Lord, don't give me any more people. I don't want to be responsible for any more people."

Robinson: Have you detected patterns in friends and colleagues who've failed to endure in ministry? If so, how can those help us?

MacArthur: In 2 Corinthians 3, Paul compares the old covenant and the new covenant, talks about the fact that he's a minister of the new covenant and that the new covenant is better, and gives all the ways it's better. Then he comes in chapter 4 and says, "Having this ministry by the mercy of God, we do not lose heart" (2 Cor. 4:1). Ministry is a mercy. It's an undeserved mercy. That means I don't deserve it. I couldn't earn it. So why would I walk away from it if it doesn't satisfy me? It is a mercy that I'm even in the ministry.... I think Paul sees it as a mercy, and he suffered.

He suffered and not only from things on the outside but even worse, for the care of the churches. It was a life of suffering because he was so burdened by their process of sanctification being halted so frequently by false teachers and other things. I think if you're going to endure in the ministry, you have to understand that being called to minister God's Word is a mercy; it is such an incredible privilege that you need to take it for what it is and not ask for more. The Lord has probably given you all he's gifted you to handle.

Robinson: Let's say I'm a seminary student training for pastoral ministry or a brand-new pastor serving in my first vocational ministry position—how would you advise me to avoid the many pitfalls that threaten me both as a Christian and as a pastor?

MacArthur: Let's assume you're going to teach the Scriptures, let's assume that's in your commitment. I would say this: love your people. To be able to survive fifty years, five decades, and not crash and burn and not develop animosity or disappointment in people, love them. You know the real work of the Holy Spirit in the life of a believer is to produce love, joy, peace, gentleness, goodness, faith, meekness, self-control. All those things need to be manifestly evident in the life of a pastor so he can survive.

If you don't have those graces in your life by the Holy Spirit, you're not going to survive. One of two things is going to happen. Either you're going to go, or the people are going to go, and you're going to be in a revolving-door church. You're going to bring them in the back door with whatever you're doing and run them right out the side door eventually after they get to know you. So the one thing I'd say is take heed to yourself and to your doctrine. And by that I mean, let those people know that you give your life for them because you love them.

I'm holding in my arms the great-grandchild of the people I ministered to first. The families love me, and they love my wife, Patricia, and they love our family and our kids and our grandkids. There has to be integrity in your life, so take heed to yourself. The only way you can survive is by walking in the Spirit and having the Spirit manifest his fruit in your life. I'd say the proof of the character of a church is not in its ability to attract young people. It's in its ability to hold old people. That's the character of a church.

If you asked me what marks Grace Church, I would say this: generations of people in the same families who love their church, who embrace their church in every way, who give generously, constantly, who serve, volunteer, fellowship, worship. That kind of endurance doesn't come from a program. It comes from an affection that runs deep between a shepherd and his people, and it's tested at every possible level through those decades. The end result and fruit of it is the richest of all spiritual experiences for the pastor and his people. But not many men experience that.

Contributors

Tom Ascol is senior pastor of Grace Baptist Church in Cape Coral, Florida, and executive director of Founders Ministries.

D. A. Carson is president of the Gospel Coalition and also served as a professor of New Testament at Trinity Evangelical Divinity School in Deerfield, Illinois, for forty years.

Bryan Chapell is senior pastor of Grace Presbyterian Church (PCA) in Peoria, Illinois, and is a council member with the Gospel Coalition.

Dan Doriani is vice president of strategic academic projects and professor of theology and ethics at Covenant Theological Seminary in St. Louis, Missouri, and is a council member with the Gospel Coalition.

Collin Hansen is editorial director for the Gospel Coalition and serves on the advisory board of Beeson Divinity School.

Dave Harvey is executive director of Sojourn Network, teaching pastor at Summit Church in Fort Myers / Naples, Florida, and founder of Am I Called?

Tim Keller is the founding pastor of Redeemer Presbyterian Church (PCA) in Manhattan, chairman of Redeemer City to City, and vice president of the Gospel Coalition.

Mark McCullough is senior pastor of First Baptist Church of Frisco City, Alabama.

Scott Patty is the founding pastor of Grace Community Church in Nashville, Tennessee.

Jeff Robinson Sr. is pastor of Christ Fellowship Church of Louisville, Kentucky, and is a senior editor for the Gospel Coalition.

Juan R. Sanchez is senior pastor of High Pointe Baptist Church in Austin, Texas, and a council member with the Gospel Coalition.

Brandon Shields is pastor of Soma Church in Indianapolis, Indiana.

John Starke is lead pastor at Apostles Church Uptown in New York City.

General Index

Scripture Index

THE GOSPEL **COALITION**

The Gospel Coalition is a fellowship of evangelical churches deeply committed to renewing our faith in the gospel of Christ and to reforming our ministry practices to conform fully to the Scriptures. We have committed ourselves to invigorating churches with new hope and compelling joy based on the promises received by grace alone through faith alone in Christ alone.

We desire to champion the gospel with clarity, compassion, courage, and joy—gladly linking hearts with fellow believers across denominational, ethnic, and class lines. We yearn to work with all who, in addition to embracing our confession and theological vision for ministry, seek the lordship of Christ over the whole of life with unabashed hope in the power of the Holy Spirit to transform individuals, communities, and cultures.

Through its pastoral resources, The Gospel Coalition aims to encourage and equip current and prospective pastors for faithful endurance over a lifetime of ministry in the church. By learning from experienced ministers of different ages, races, and nationalities, we hope to grow together in godly maturity as the Spirit leads us in the way of Jesus Christ.

Join the cause and visit TGC.org for fresh resources that will equip you to love God with all your heart, soul, mind, and strength, and to love your neighbor as yourself.

TGC.org

Also Available from the Gospel Coalition

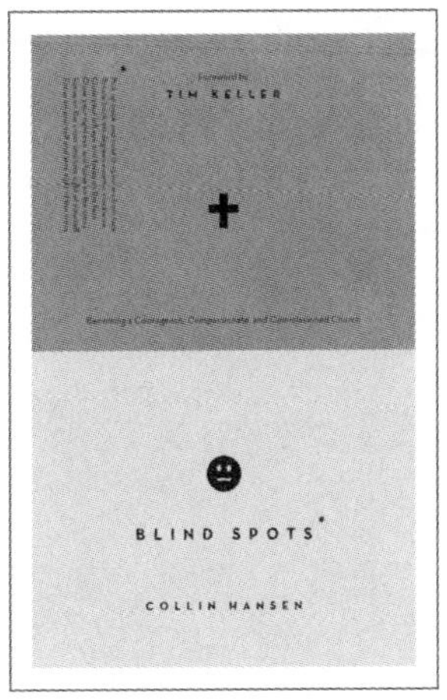

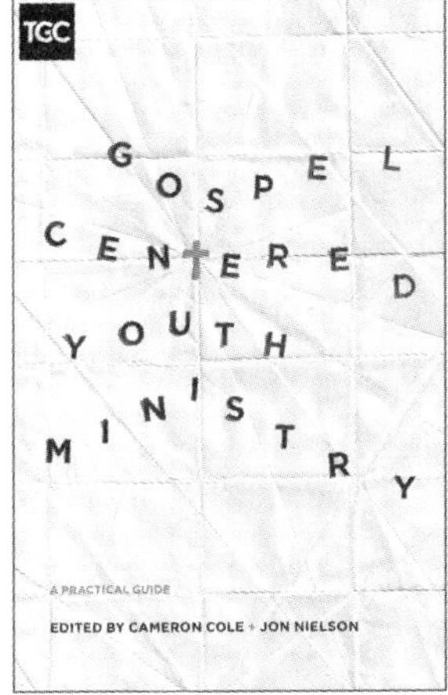

For more information, visit **crossway.org**.